THE BIG PICTURE

WHAT CANADIANS THINK
ABOUT ALMOST EVERYTHING

ALLAN GREGG AND MICHAEL POSNER

MACFARLANE WALTER & ROSS
TORONTO

Canadian Cataloguing in Publication Data
Gregg, Allan R.
    The big picture: what Canadians think about almost everything

ISBN 0-921912-11-0

1. Public opinion – Canada.   2. Canada – Social conditions – 1971- – Public opinion.   3. Canada – Politics and government – 1980-1984 – Public opinion.*   4. Canada – Politics and government – 1984- – Public opinion.*   5. Canadians – Attitudes.
I. Posner, Michael, 1947-   II. Title.

HM261.G74 1990   971.064'7   C90-095037-4

FIRST EDITION

Macfarlane Walter & Ross
37A Hazelton Avenue
Toronto, Canada M5R 2E3

Printed and bound in Canada

To the men and women of Decima who have toiled in anonymity while I received the applause. It is my hope that this book brings them the recognition they so much deserve.

ARG

In memory of Sam and Rhea, who taught me love for the printed word.

MSP

CONTENTS

ACKNOWLEDGMENTS

THIS BOOK WAS LITERALLY TEN YEARS IN THE MAKING. MORE THAN most, therefore, it is the product of a broad coalition of extraordinary talent and energy.

We are particularly indebted to Rick Anderson for his early pioneering efforts in getting the *Decima Quarterly Report* off the ground; to Charles Fremes, for his dedication to professionalism and quality; to Carole Schnell, for her constant support and friendship over the last ten years; to Marjorie Macpherson, for her insightful analysis of the *Quarterly*; to Chris Kelly, for his support and encouragement; to Jill Heron and Roberta Grant, for their prodigious efforts at research; to David Groskind, for his patience in dealing with technological cretinism; to Jim Ireland and Peter Enneson, for creating a graphic vision faithful to the text; and to Ivon Owen, for his perceptive and fastidious copy editing. We must single out John Macfarlane, who edited the manuscript with his always scrupulous concern for excellence; and his colleagues, Jan Walter, for her enthusiastic commitment to the project; and Gary Ross, whose inspiration this work was.

A NOTE ON METHODOLOGY

THE DECIMA QUARTERLY REPORT CONTAINS THE RESULTS OF 1,500 interviews conducted by telephone with a representative national sample of Canadian citizens, eighteen years of age or older. It employs a multi-stage, systematic, random sampling technique which produces results projected to the entire population accurate within plus or minus 2.6 percentage points 95 times out of 100. In order to provide an adequate sample to describe each region individually, over-sampling is undertaken in specific sampling strata. To project the results on a national basis, each sub-sample is weighted to reflect its actual contribution to population. Interviews are conducted in both official languages from five central locations. Approximately 15 percent of the interviews are independently validated before being edited, coded, and processed. Surveying for the *Quarterly* is conducted four times a year; field work is undertaken in March, June, September, and December.

The data in this book is taken from the *Quarterly Report*, 1980-1990, and from Decima surveys conducted for *Maclean's* magazine through the decade.

INTRODUCTION

"The world is not run by thought, nor by imagination, but by opinion. "

ELIZABETH DREW

IN 1980, CANADIAN LEADERS LAMENTED THE CANADIAN PUBLIC'S unrealistic expectations. They saw a population that believed salary demands, no matter how high, could be met; that spent beyond its means; that believed government could solve all its problems; and that failed to recognize the need to balance private interests and the public good. As the decade began, Canadians still clung to a post-war ethos which held that progress was normal – that the next house would be bigger, the next car faster, the next paycheque fatter.

The public, of course, saw things differently from their leaders. Their lament was for what they considered the country's squandered potential. They acknowledged the country's problems, but saw them as aberrations, as problems they didn't deserve: problems that, given resolve and leadership, could be solved. To be told that their expectations were unrealistic was the thin end of a wedge that would divide the Canadian people from their leaders throughout the decade. The Progressive Conservative Party's 1979 campaign theme recognized this growing chasm. It asked simply: "Do you want four more years like the last eleven?" Prior to the election almost 90% of Canadians responded with a resounding "No!"

As we entered the 1980s, our post-war values were challenged by changing experience. Inflation was eroding real income.

Our dollar, no longer pegged to the American buck, had fallen to 84 cents U.S. And for the first time in Canadian history, home ownership in major urban centres eluded the grasp of the middle class. But rather than abandon traditional values, Canadians chose to reassess the traditional means of realizing them. Rather than abandon the belief that education was the key to success, they concluded that something must be wrong with the educational system. Rather than abandon the belief that government could solve all problems, they concluded that government was badly run and the nation's political leaders to blame.

The process of reassessment was personal as well as public. As inflation eroded wages, we saw an increased demand for non-salary benefits – job training, a safer and more enjoyable work environment, a four-day work week. People who felt the dream of home ownership slipping away were buying designer clothes, prime cuts of meat, and exotic stereo equipment. Canadians began to adjust their life styles to accommodate a growing sense of "abnormalcy."

The economic recession of 1981-82 simply heightened and exaggerated the trend. While Canadians clung tenaciously to their traditional belief that "if you work hard and put your mind to it you can be anything you want in Canada," two-thirds reported concern that in the near future either they or the main income-earner might be out of work. Still committed to the belief that "Canada is the best country in the world in which to live," only 18% reported satisfaction with the direction in which the country was headed. And while more than 75% held steadfastly to the view that governments could at least partially, if not totally, solve the problem that concerned them most, Decima polls recorded the lowest levels of satisfaction ever accorded a central government in the Western world.

The recession traumatized the Canadian people. They came to the conclusion that "the old rules no longer work." Decima referred to this phenomenon as "the post-recession survivors mentality." While they didn't enjoy the recession or the trauma it induced, people believed it had taught them lessons that would serve them well in the future. And, like all survivors, they said, "Never again."

The most remarkable manifestation of the post-recession survivors mentality was a disenchantment with government involvement in the private sector. One of the hallmarks of Canadian culture has been a collectivist impulse that embraces the notion that government must not only arbitrate on behalf of the public interest, but, if necessary, provide it. The history of the CPR, the centralization of our banking system, the existence of publicly owned airlines, broadcasting and oil companies – all were expressions of this sentiment. However, by the summer of 1982, two-thirds of Canadians were persuaded that government intervention in the private sector had increased, and the majority of them felt that this growth in intervention had hindered rather than helped the economy. Comparative data showed that more Canadians than Americans felt that business rather than government was best able to represent their economic interests.

Like the belief that "the old rules don't work," this appraisal of the proper role of government was pragmatic rather than ideological. Government intervention had been the prescribed (indeed, the approved) solution to problems which worsened and grew more complex, so Canadians concluded that there must be another answer. But this pro-business bias was not without qualifications. It was not, as many thought at the time, a wholesale call for the withdrawal of government from the economy. Rather, it proposed a more discreet and less intrusive role: government as a catalyst rather than an initiator; government as a facilitator rather than a regulator; government as a planner and rule-setter rather than a doer and a play-maker.

And there was a corollary: expecting less from government, people were prepared to take more responsibility for their own lives. The flip side of our historical collectivist impulse was an absence of faith in the individual – a sentiment best expressed by the view, "I can't really do very much to solve our problems, but society's major institutions can." Surprisingly, Canadians did not emerge from the recession feeling downtrodden or put upon. On the contrary, 1983 surveys revealed an unprecedented sense of powerfulness and personal efficacy. Canadians had a new faith in themselves. They felt they could now take matters into their own hands.

This renewed sense of individual worth laid the foundations for social bonding, a process in which like-minded individuals get together to tackle problems unaddressed by traditional authorities.

In the recession's wake we saw the growth of voluntarism, single-interest and activist groups. At the same time, we saw the loss of unquestioned faith in advertising, politicians, and religious leaders.

Another distinguishing characteristic of Canadian society has been our insularity. This, too, changed profoundly during the 1980s. The prospect of nuclear war, the demands for disarmament, and the sight of American troops invading Grenada shocked Canada into an awakening of international consciousness. These events drew us to the inescapable conclusion that, no matter how much we might wish otherwise, we could not escape the fallout from world events. This, in turn, changed our views of ourselves. Recognizing our place in the world, we grew more acutely aware of our common North American destiny.

As we became more outward-looking, we began to ask ourselves what role we could play in a North American context. Acknowledging the improbability of our ever becoming a military or economic leader, we defined ourselves increasingly in terms of what the United States was not: where it was warlike, we were peaceable; where it was strong-willed, we were tolerant; where it was mean-spirited, we were charitable. Against the conventional wisdom about our inferiority complex, the 1980s saw Canada develop a sense of superiority. If not a military or economic leader, Canada would be a moral leader. If we were to lead, it would be by example.

The recession, while not forgotten, was now behind us. Armed with a renewed sense of confidence and worth, on the one hand, and a belief in the efficacy of "the new rules," on the other, Canadians were in no mood to suffer stewards of the status quo. Against this background, the election of the Progressive Conservatives – an opposition party, railing against the old rules, advocating a less interventionist, more pro-business posture – seemed almost inevitable. Even with a new leader, the Liberals were seen to be defending an approach which the public now associated more with problems than solutions. By 1984, Canada's "national governing party" was caught in the vice-grip of changing public opinion.

It was out with the old and in with the new. The Liberals now sat in opposition; the Tories now occupied the seats of power. The nation was more confident in 1985 than at any other time in the decade, but its optimisim was relatively short-lived. While Canadians believed the economy was improving, they began to worry that the fruits of this renewed prosperity were not being shared equally. The West, in particular, had a keen sense that the benefits of economic recovery were being reaped disproportionately in Central Canada. Quebec, on the other hand, bristled with new-found confidence. Instead of church and state, Quebeckers turned to "la P.M.E." (la petite et moyenne entreprise) as the new expression of their cultural nationalism and pride. Bombardier and Provigo became household names, and the most over-subscribed department in the most over-subscribed university became McGill's school of business.

This growing sense of disparity existed among classes as well as regions. In a country where virtually everyone felt he belonged or could aspire to the middle class, lower-income earners now viewed their circumstances as permanent and immutable, calling upon government not to improve their lot but simply to protect them. The view that Canada was made up of "haves" and "have nots" clouded the otherwise bright outlook of the mid-1980s. It also meant that fairness, more than effectiveness, became the test by which the public measured new initiatives. It was not surprising that the Progressive Conservatives' first budget, which proposed "deindexing" the pensions of senior citizens, met with howls of outrage.

Even as confidence in the economy grew throughout 1986 and 1987, public optimism declined dramatically. Canadians were hoping for the best, but they were planning for the worst. This was, in part, a hangover from the recession. The most memorable of the lessons we learned during the period of "abnormalcy" was that we should remain vigilant. Declining optimism in the face of continued and acknowledged economic improvement was a defence mechanism. But there was more to it than that. Whereas in the early 1980s Canadians saw change as a necessity, by 1987 many of us found the prospect of change overwhelming. When people said they believed the country would experience more change in the next two years than in the last ten, it was with a sense not of excitement and expectancy but of dread.

Decima referred to this tendency as "millennial anxiety": people peered into the next century and were certain that many things they took for granted ten years earlier were now at risk. In one survey 44% of Canadians believed that in the year 2001 they would be unable to drink water out of the tap; 75% doubted they would be able to buy a house in the urban core. In short, Canadians were approaching the future rootless and rudderless.

This was the backdrop against which the battle of free trade was waged. Public opinion divided, not simply on the supposed merits or drawbacks of the proposed free-trade agreement, but even more starkly on attitudes toward the future. People who were confident about Canada's prospects – who felt insulated from the perils of the millennium – supported free trade; people who were more fearful – who felt vulnerable in society – opposed it. Small wonder the Progressive Conservatives entered the 1988 election attempting to avoid the issue head on, claiming the real question was "who was best able to manage change."

Free trade made the headlines, but this shift in outlook had more profound implications. At the root of millennial anxiety was a crash of expectations – a view that progress, far from being normal, might be a thing of the past; and that tomorrow, far from being better, might be worse than today. If the recession had traumatized Canadians, this crash of expectations now sobered us up. As the decade drew to a close, upper- and lower-income Canadians came to the same conclusion: that there was more to life than money and the things it would buy.

This may be the most significant change in public opinion in modern history, because it marks a departure from quantity of life and an emphasis on "more" to quality of life and an emphasis on "better." It suggests that the growing environmental awareness of the late 1980s is not only permanent but perhaps only the tip of an iceberg. The 1990s may witness the ascendancy of a whole basket of social concerns ranging from health and fitness to crime and drugs.

We left the decade seeking a "quieter and gentler" life. But we begin our quest without solid clues as to how to achieve our new aspirations and without a strong belief that the past will provide any useful lessons. Our faith in traditional leaders has never been lower. Our sense of how to go about forging a common destiny and purpose has never been more diffuse. As we look to the 1990s, it appears the wisdom of public opinion will be borne out once again: Canada will face more change in the next two years than it has in the last ten.

WHO ARE WE?

CHAPTER 1

"It is perhaps a unique characteristic of civilization that each civilization believes in its uniqueness and its superiority to other civilizations. Indeed, this may be the meaning of culture – i.e., something which we have that others have not."

HAROLD INNIS, 1951

"I cannot see why America should have such a terrible effect on Canada. I want to see Canada develop her special form of culture, her special political forms, deal with the great problems of the world and set a good example to the world. I cannot see why Canada cannot do that perfectly. One doesn't want to make her the richest and most luxurious city in the world, but a state of the best citizens and that is what she can do."

ST. LOE STRACHEY, EDITOR OF THE *SPECTATOR*, 1925

"You can be a French Canadian or an English Canadian, but not a Canadian. We know how to live without an identity, and this is one of our marvellous resources."

MARSHALL MCLUHAN, 1967

IT WAS IN THE 1980S THAT THE MYTH OF CANADA'S INFERIORITY complex was finally and irrevocably shattered. When we compared ourselves to the nation with which we shared a continent, the nation in whose orbit we forever seemed to have travelled, the nation against whom we naturally measured ourselves and our achievements, we were not worse: we were better. Or so we thought.

CONSTITUTIONAL ANXIETY   As the Meech Lake controversy limped toward
its dramatic finale in June 1990, increasing numbers of Canadians
expressed uncertainty about the Accord – and the future of the country.

"Canadians are no longer not-Americans. We have evolved into a people who are as fully North Americans as are Americans and yet who, because of our political culture, are now a quite distinct kind of North American....Here, two nations have evolved that are utterly alike in almost all of their externals and yet are utterly unalike in their political cultures so that they are as distinct from each other as the Germans from the French."

RICHARD GWYN, IN *THE 49TH PARADOX*, 1985

The Americans sent their young men to fight in Vietnam, Grenada, Panama; Canada sent its soldiers on United Nations missions aimed at preventing war. Who was more peaceable? American cities had race riots and black ghettos; Canadians knew nothing of that. Who was more tolerant? Americans paid small fortunes in medical-insurance premiums; every Canadian had access to low-cost medicare. Who was more charitable? It did not matter that Americans had B-1 bombers and we did not. Nor did it matter that the American economy was at least ten times as large as our own. The issue wasn't size and power; it was morality. And in our own minds at least, we were a morally superior people.

It was the late George Grant who wrote that "to think of the United States is to think of ourselves – almost." But "almost" is a very large territory. Surveys throughout the decade reveal that Canadians think of themselves as far less violent than Americans – as well as harder-working, less competitive, better informed, more concerned about the environment and the disadvantaged, and generally more honest. And we fear that the stronger economic ties implicit in the U.S.-Canada free-trade agreement may make us more like Americans – eroding that sense of what makes Canada special.

Nearly three-quarters of Canadians believed in December 1985 that our culture and identity were different from that of the United States. Respondents cite our relations with other countries, our history and geography, our treatment of minorities, our political system and the arts as central components of that distinct identity. But we also recognize that it is our linguistic duality that chiefly distinguishes us from Americans.

Collectively, we think of ourselves as tolerant, peaceful, and independent. Americans think of themselves in much the same way, although they stress independence far more than tolerance or peacefulness. The real differences lie in our views about each other. Americans genuinely seem to like Canadians. Our most striking characteristic, they say, is friendliness; in one survey, 50% described us as either friendly, neighbourly, nice, wonderful, or delightful. More Americans would like to live in Canada than would Canadians in the United States. And Americans who are asked what it is they like least about Canadians are most inclined to say simply "nothing."

But ask a Canadian to choose adjectives describing Americans and the characterizations are far less generous. Some 29% in March 1989 used the words "pig-headed, obnoxious, aggressive, snobs, or stupid." And while we clearly regard ourselves as the superior society, 25% of us say the worst aspect of Americans is their superiority complex.

On two issues – the state of our relative economies and levels of taxation – large numbers of Canadians concede that the American way is stronger or better. But 67% of us think our overall quality of life is better than Americans'; another 62% think Canada is more respected in the world than is the United States; and 89% maintain that our system of universal medical care is significantly better. Not surprisingly, most Canadians want to preserve the independence that confers these benefits. In a March 1989 survey, 85% opposed the notion of Canada's becoming the 51st state; 49% rejected having a common currency; and 60% dismissed the idea of the two countries' taking a united line on defence and foreign-policy issues.

Underpinning this national pride was confidence in our ability to solve economic problems. In the 1980s, large majorities of Canadians agreed that we had the potential and resources to grapple with economic issues – although the actual level of agreement declined to 83% during the recession and, significantly, continued to weaken as the decade wore on.

In fact, in our own minds, Canada was the best country in the world in which to live. An overwhelming majority of respondents endorsed that proposition throughout the decade; the actual numbers were as high as 93% in 1989 and never lower than 79%, during the 1982 recession. Older, less educated females living in rural or smaller centres were most supportive of the Canada-is-the-best-nation thesis. Younger, more affluent urban Canadians – especially Quebeckers – were less likely to support it.

Attempting to identify the sources of this superiority complex, Decima asked Canadians to say what it was that made Canada "the best country in the world in which to live." In September 1987, fully 90% said it was the quality and availability of health care. A slightly smaller majority (78% in March 1988) thought it was our education system. While concern about pollution rose dramatically in the 1980s, 76% said in June 1989

FACTS

According to Statistics Canada, there were 24.04 million Canadians in January 1980 and 26.09 million in January 1989.

In 1987, Canada's population (25.6 million) constituted .5% of the world's total.

From 1981 to 1986, Canada's population grew by 4.2%, the lowest rate of growth in more than 100 years.

Rank of Canada by size among countries of the world: 2 (the Soviet Union is 1)
Rank of Canada by population among countries of the world: 31

Size of Canada in square kilometres: just under 10 million
Percentage that is uninhabited: 89

"My generation of Canadians grew up believing that, if we were very good or very smart, or both, we would one day *graduate* from Canada."

ROBERT FULFORD, 1970

said in June 1989 that it was our clean environment. There was also a majority at that time – 74% – that said it was the way we welcomed immigrants of different races, religions and cultures into our society. And there was a majority too – 63% in September 1989 – that agreed that Canada's system of government made it the best place to live. (Again, agreement had weakened noticeably by the end of the decade.)

Other Canadians believed that our bilingual culture helped make Canada the best place to live – 47% in June 1988. But fully 40% did not, a remarkably high number given that bilingualism is widely thought to lie at the core of the Canadian identity. That almost one in 10 Canadians could voice no opinion on this question made the absence of consensus that much clearer. And once more, levels of agreement declined as the years passed, even in Quebec, where support had been highest. In fact, by 1988 a majority of Canadians in British Columbia and the prairie provinces rejected the suggestion that bilingualism played any role in our professed superiority – and said having one language would make Canada a better country.

The value people place on bilingualism affects views on related language issues. Those who do not regard a two-language culture as essentially Canadian are less willing to grant Quebec its constitutional claim to distinct-society status. They are also more likely to believe the rights of Quebec's anglophone minority have not been adequately protected.

The growing divide over language rights was clearly visible by the spring of 1989; 76% of Canadians expressed opposition to Bill 178, the Quebec law – passed in December 1988 – that required signs outside stores and buildings in the province to use the French language only. Majorities said the bill would hurt Canada's francophone minorities, inflame anti-French sentiments, fuel the separatist cause, and reduce investment in Quebec. More critically, Bill 178 may have marked a national watershed on the Meech Lake constitutional accord – the issue that gripped the country as we entered the 1990s. Nearly 60% of Canadians said the legislation would damage the chances of the accord's being accepted by all 10 provinces.

Significantly, only 36% of Quebeckers shared this view; for the majority in Quebec, Bill 178 was simply an

A PROUD NATION

Canada is the best country in
the world in which to live

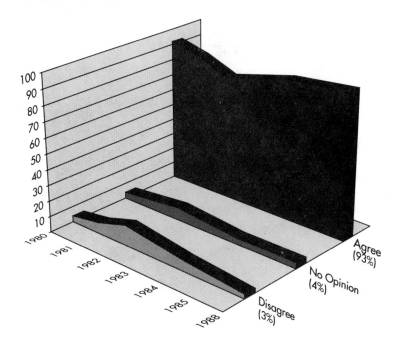

The life expectancy
of a Canadian
male in 1981:
71.88 years
In 1986: 73.02
Of a Canadian female
in 1981: 78.98
In 1986: 79.79
Province with highest
life expectancies for
both sexes in 1986:
British Columbia –
for men 73.96, for
women 80.40
Provinces with the
lowest: Quebec –
for men, 71.95;
Newfoundland –
for women: 79.06

Infant-mortality rate
per 1,000 population
in 1981: 9.6
In 1987: 7.3
Province with
the highest:
Saskatchewan – 9.7
Province with
the lowest:
Ontario – 6.6

1980 APRIL

Terry Fox begins his
Marathon of Hope in
Newfoundland. Fox,
22, who had lost a
leg to cancer, intended
to run across the
country, but ended
the run after 5,300
kilometres in Sept-
ember in Thunder
Bay, Ont., when
cancer was found in
his lungs. He died the
following year.

1980 JUNE

Parliament passes
the National Anthem
Act, making "O
Canada" the national
anthem. Two repeti-
tions of "Stand on
guard for thee," a
phrase used five
times in the original
version, are deleted
and replaced with
new phrases.

1980 OCT.

The National Energy
Program is announced
by the Liberal govern-
ment. It aims to give
Canadians 50%
control of the oil and
gas industry by 1990.

"Does it seem to you that I am talking about a nation of losers, exiles and refugees? Modern Canada is a prosperous country, but the miseries of its earliest white inhabitants are bred in the bone and cannot even now be rooted out of the flesh."

ROBERTSON DAVIES, 1988

CAN WE COPE?

Canada has the potential and resources to solve its own economic problems

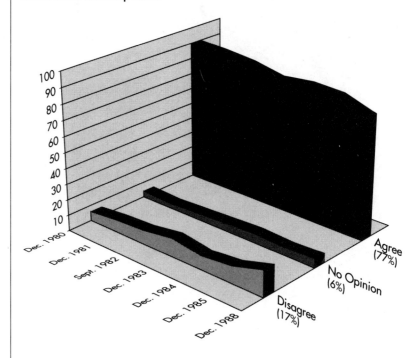

| **1980** | DEC.
Marshall McLuhan, who forecast the birth of an electronic, global village, dies. | **1981** | JUNE
The official census reports that there are 24,343,181 Canadians. | **1981** | DEC.
A TV network for the Northwest Territories begins operation, broadcasting in Inuktitut. |

HOW TOLERANT ARE WE?

One of the best things about Canada is the way
we welcome people of different races, religions
and cultures into our society

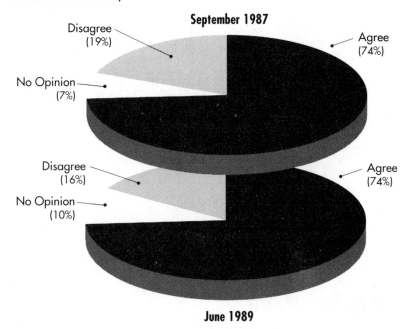

September 1987

Disagree
(19%)

Agree
(74%)

No Opinion
(7%)

Disagree
(16%)

Agree
(74%)

No Opinion
(10%)

June 1989

ARE WE BETTER FOR BEING BILINGUAL?

One of the things that makes Canada the best country
in the world in which to live is having two official
languages, English and French

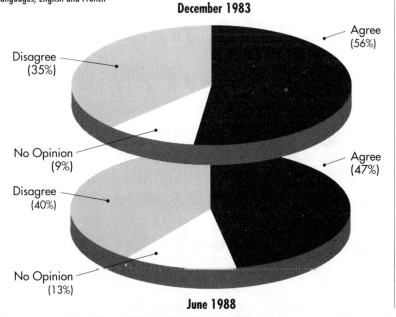

December 1983

Disagree
(35%)

Agree
(56%)

No Opinion
(9%)

Disagree
(40%)

Agree
(47%)

No Opinion
(13%)

June 1988

"There are six million more savings accounts in Canada than there are people."

ANDREW MALCOLM, *NEW YORK TIMES* REPORTER, 1988

POPULATION BY PROVINCE*

Newfoundland:	1980 – 564,600	1988 – 566,700
Prince Edward Island:	1980 – 122,500	1988 – 128,200
Nova Scotia:	1980 – 843,700	1988 – 880,300
New Brunswick:	1980 – 693,900	1988 – 712,300
Quebec:	1980 – 6,359,900	1988 – 6,618,600
Ontario:	1980 – 8,539,800	1988 – 9,368,200
Manitoba:	1980 – 1,023,000	1988 – 1,080,900
Saskatchewan:	1980 – 955,500	1988 – 1,012,800
Alberta:	1980 – 2,105,600	1988 – 2,318,600
British Columbia:	1980 – 2,636,400	1988 – 2,960,900
Yukon:	1980 – 22,600	1988 – 24,900
Northwest Territories:	1980 – 44,300	1988 – 51,900

*1988 figures are preliminary estimates

THE GREAT DIVIDE

One of the things that makes Canada the best country in the world in which to live is having two official languages, English and French.

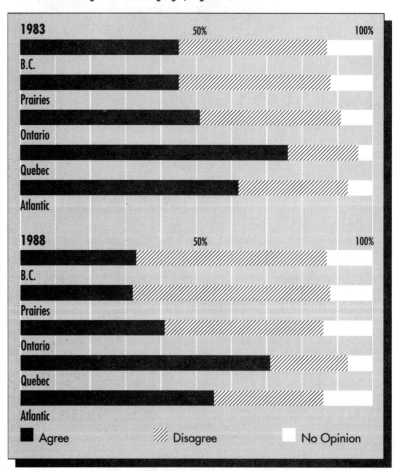

By December 1989, most Canadians said the fundamental problem with the Accord was that it increased the powers of the Quebec government.

The resentment of Quebec, particularly in Western Canada, was evident even before the provincial premiers signed the original Meech Lake document in 1987. Westerners regarded the Accord as yet another federal surrender to Quebec. In September 1989, 49% of all Canadians endorsed the statement: "I'm tired of giving special treatment to French-speaking residents of Quebec." Westerners were the most likely to agree. They were also the least likely to support giving Quebec constitutional recognition as a distinct society; and the most likely to dismiss the importance of getting Quebec's agreement to the constitution – and the importance of Meech Lake itself.

The acrimony over Meech raised serious questions about the strength of Canada's 123-year-old confederation. A majority said the controversy had done more to rupture national unity than it had to cement it (although 60% were not convinced that the failure to ratify the accord would tear the country apart). Most Canadians do not want Quebec to separate, but the country is divided about what it should do if separation is threatened; almost as many would want to let the province go as would try to change its mind.

The collapse of the Meech Lake Accord clearly adds a new, more troubling dimension to the period of introspection that Canadians are about to enter. Our basic identity once consisted in part of our bilingual culture: it helped define us as a nation; it made us unique. The prospect of a Canada without Quebec, or even of some new, still undefined constitutional arrangement short of separation, clearly raises profound questions – if not about who we are, then about who we will become. In the long debate over the merits of Meech Lake, critics of the Accord complained frequently of francophonic fatigue: they were weary of the seemingly endless discussions of national unity. The irony, of course, is that Meech's death guarantees that Canadians will be discussing national unity for much of the uncertain decade to come.

FACTS

Number of deaths per 100,000 population from diseases of the circulatory system in 1970: among men 431.5; among women 351.7
Number in 1980: among men 354.6; among women 277.1
Number in 1987: among men 277.5; among women 218.9

Number of deaths per 100,000 population from ischemic heart disease in 1970: among men 297.7; among women 200.2
In 1980: among men 232.8; among women 150.9
In 1987: among men 179.7; among women 118.2

Number of deaths per 100,000 population from cancer in 1975-77: among men 170.9; among women 128.6
In 1985-87: among men 182.1; among women 125.6

INTO THE NINETIES

If it is true that Canadians think of themselves as superior to Americans, and of our way of life as superior to the American way of life, then Canadians are likely to face a crisis of identity in the 1990s. At a minimum, we will undergo a period of intense introspection. The reason: our self-image is no longer consonant with reality. We may believe that we are more tolerant, more charitable, more humane than Americans, but experience suggests that in many respects we are almost identical. In the decade ahead, that dissonance is likely to provoke a re-examination of the kind of people we have become – and what we must do to become the kind of people we would like to be.

What made Canadians distinct in the 1980s was that we weren't Americans – and we were proud of it. We genuinely believed that we treated our poor and disadvantaged better, that our health-care system was superior, that our laws protecting the environment were tougher. (In fact, they often weren't.) Cultural nationalists decried the influence of *Miami Vice* and other American television imports, but such shows never threatened Canada's identity; they reinforced it. We knew that Canadian policemen didn't drive sports cars and wear Armani suits. Canadian policemen drove dull cars and wore dull clothes. Whatever else *Miami Vice* may have been, it was not a depiction of anything remotely Canadian. We were not like that: we were better.

But as we enter the 1990s, that moral edge is eroding. We view the quality of life, which underpins our superiority complex, as increasingly threatened by crime in the streets, unsafe neighbourhoods, illegal drugs, racism, environmental degradation. The 1990s will be marked by a sober reassessment of what has gone wrong – largely in our cities, where most of us live – and a search for solutions that will change our relationship with the rest of the world.

Canadian culture was once remarkably insular. Having no great effect on the world, we believed that the world had no great effect on us. But the 1980s brought a genuine awakening of international consciousness, a recognition that events in the Sahel or the Amazonian rain forests or Eastern Europe have an impact in Canada.

THE IMPACT OF FREE TRADE

How will free trade affect Canada's ability to
maintain its independence and identity?

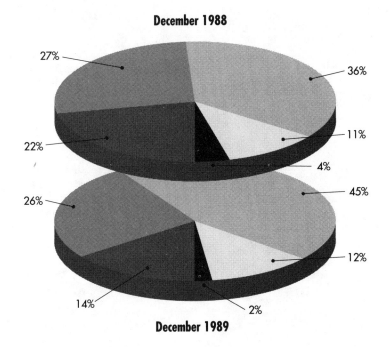

December 1988

27%
36%
22%
11%
4%

December 1989

26%
45%
14%
12%
2%

 Help a Great Deal   ■ Hurt a Great Deal   ▨ No Impact

■ No Opinion   ■ Hurt Somewhat   ▨ Help Somewhat

FACTS

Percentage of population 15 years and older in 1987 that has completed elementary school: 17.8 Percentage that has completed high school: 49

Percentage of Canadians in 1981 who said their mother tongue was English: 61.28 Percentage who said it was French: 25.67 Percentage who said it was Italian: 1.8 Percentage who said it was German: 1.73

Percentage of Canadians in 1986 who said their mother tongue was English: 60.6 Percentage who said French: 24.3 Percentage who said Italian: 1.8 Percentage who said German: 1.7

1982 OCT.	**1983** JUNE	**1984** MAY
Dominion Day officially becomes Canada Day.	The U.S. space shuttle uses the made-in-Canada "Canadarm" to release and retrieve a satellite in space.	The Supreme Court of Canada issues its first judgment on the Charter of Rights and Freedoms, ruling that an Ontario law requiring lawyers to be citizens of Canada is not unconstitutional.
Mountain climbers Laurie Skreslet of Calgary and Patrick Morrow of Kimberly, B.C., become the first Canadians to scale Mt. Everest.		

"National identity is the quintessential Canadian issue. Almost alone among modern developed countries, Canada has continued to debate its self-conception to the present day....There is no ideology of Canadianism."

SEYMOUR MARTIN LIPSET, 1990

QUEBEC'S LANGUAGE LAW

What effect will Bill 178, Quebec's language law, have?

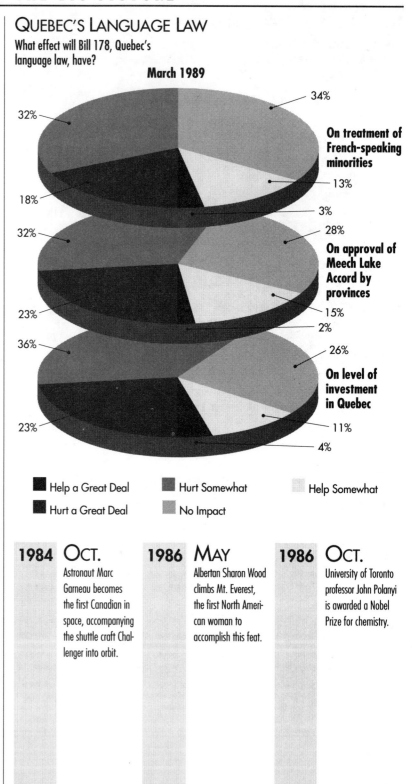

March 1989

On treatment of French-speaking minorities
- 34%
- 13%
- 3%
- 32%
- 18%

On approval of Meech Lake Accord by provinces
- 28%
- 15%
- 2%
- 32%
- 23%

On level of investment in Quebec
- 26%
- 11%
- 4%
- 36%
- 23%

■ Help a Great Deal   ■ Hurt Somewhat   ▨ Help Somewhat
■ Hurt a Great Deal   ▨ No Impact

1984 OCT.	**1986** MAY	**1986** OCT.
Astronaut Marc Garneau becomes the first Canadian in space, accompanying the shuttle craft Challenger into orbit.	Albertan Sharon Wood climbs Mt. Everest, the first North American woman to accomplish this feat.	University of Toronto professor John Polanyi is awarded a Nobel Prize for chemistry.

COMPARATIVE DATA

Number of Canadian police officers per 100,000 population in 1981: 220

Number in the United States: 386

Number in Canada in 1985: 210

Number in the United States in 1985: 422

Percentage of Americans in 1985 who said they believed in the devil: 66

Percentage of anglophone Canadians: 46

Percentage of francophone Canadians: 25

Percentage of Canadians who belong to the Baptist Church: 3

Percentage of Americans: 20

Percentage of Canadians in 1986 who held stocks: 13

Percentage of Americans in 1985 who held stocks: 20

Percentage of Canadians aged 18-24 enrolled full time in colleges and universities in 1985: 14.5

Percentage of Americans: 22

Amount donated by Canadians per capita to non-religious charitable institutions in 1985: $122

Amount donated by Americans: $180 (US)

FACTS

**Net migration in 1981, per 1,000 population: 2.5
In 1987: 4.3
Net migration is the difference between the number of immigrants and the number of emigrants.**

**Other fragments of the mosaic:
Number of Chinese Canadians: 267,000
Number of Ukrainian Canadians: 208,000
Number of Portuguese Canadians: 154,000
Number of Indo-Pakistani Canadians: 135,000
Number of Dutch Canadians: 124,000
Number of Polish Canadians: 123,000
Number of Greek Canadians: 110,000
Number of Spanish Canadians: 83,000
Number of Yugoslav Canadians: 94,000**

1987 FEB.

University of Toronto astronomer Ian Shelton discovers a supernova — the light formed by the explosion of a star. It is the first such discovery in 383 years.

1987 MAY

Wheelchair athlete Rick Hansen completes a 24,000-mile trek through 34 countries, raising $20 million for spinal-cord research, rehabilitation, and wheelchair sports.

1988 JAN.

Prime Minister Brian Mulroney and U.S. President Ronald Reagan sign the Free Trade Agreement.

"The evolution of the province of Quebec into a francophone nation-state is the unmistakable long-run message of Canadian history. It is not easy to say when the next crisis between English-speaking Canada and the francophones will occur, or what will trigger it, but that it is coming is certain."

PETER BRIMELOW, *THE PATRIOT GAME*, 1986

SHAMROCK SUMMITEERS   The first formal meeting between President Ronald Reagan and Prime Minister Brian Mulroney in March 1985 marked a shift in the direction of friendlier relations with the United States.

1988 JULY
The House of Commons passes amendments to the Official Languages Act, designed to augment bilingual services at the federal level.

1988 JULY
The 1914 War Measures Act is formally repealed. The Emergencies Act that replaces it severely limits the government's right to suspend civil liberties in the event of an emergency.

1989 JULY
The CBC all-news cable network begins broadcasting.

Interest rates, inflation and other economic barometers may once have been domestic problems that required domestic solutions. But in the 1980s, we began to understand that the major trading nations were economically interdependent and that the Canadian economy was often a victim of circumstances beyond its control – and beyond the control of any political leader.

In response to this global challenge, Canadians may become more assertive. Canada can play a role in the world, not as an economic or military leader, but as a moral leader – in human rights, in peacekeeping, perhaps even in business. It is worth remembering that in 1984, long before the debate on free trade began, 94% of Canadians thought free trade with the United States was a good idea. That statistic was more than just an overwhelming bias in favour of the accord. It implicitly acknowledged that Canada is not an island, that we must reach out, trade, and be part of the world. We need not regret our transformation from a goods-making to a service-providing economy. We don't need to manufacture television sets; we can manufacture television shows.

In the 1990s, we are likely to see more reaching out. We will continue to play the role of honest broker and peacekeeper in international affairs. But we may go further. If our political leaders were to argue, for example, that Canada has an ability – indeed, a responsibility – to become a world leader in the export of new environmental technology, Canadians would stand up and applaud. They would pressure universities and industry to find solutions that could be marketed abroad. In pursuit of moral leadership, it is possible to conceive a scenario in which Canadians willingly forgo traditional benefits in favour of environmental technology – arguing that defence budgets should be slashed dramatically in favour of more ecological research and development. Our identity need not be based on saving the world from the evils of Communism – especially since it no longer needs to be saved. But it might be based on saving the world from environmental disaster by sharing our environmental expertise.

But the question now – never mind visions of moral leadership – is how the Meech Lake constitutional wrangling will affect Canadian identity. Despite our moral superiority vis-à-vis Americans, we harbour strong resentments toward one another. Regional tensions are higher than ever before, although there is still an

FACTS

The number of bilingual Canadians increased by 27% from 1971-81, more than twice the rate of the population's growth.
In 1981, some 3.7 million Canadians said they were bilingual; 2.2 million of these were francophone, 1.1 million were anglophone.
In 1986, 4.1 million Canadians called themselves bilingual.

The Northwest Territories is the only region in Canada where neither English- nor French-Canadians dominate; aboriginal Canadians are the majority ethnic group.

emotional high ground: our affinity to the nation as a whole. An overwhelming number of Canadians continue to believe that Canada is one of the best countries in which to live, that we are richer for having two cultures, and that our multicultural traditions are worth preserving. The problem is a perception that tolerance and fairness are no longer the rules of the game. So why be fair? Why be tolerant?

We saw this most starkly in Manitoba. Its response to Meech Lake had the unmistakable aroma of revenge. In denying its assent to the accord, it was getting even for years of accumulated injury. Manitobans believed that they had been bullied in the schoolyard of Canadian politics. The federal government – ruled by a Conservative party that had pledged to end the anomalies – was, through Meech, seen to be perpetuating the status quo. Manitobans came to believe that the deck of Canadian politics was permanently stacked against them, whatever the party in power.

Nor were they alone. Much of the West is convinced that Confederation is an elaborate conspiracy designed to prevent it from playing its rightful role in national affairs. In the 1970s, Westerners envied the East; by the 1980s, they knew better. They, too, had resources, money, talent – but the Liberals refused to let them into the game. Now, with the Tories in power, nothing has changed. The West is still misunderstood in central Canada. It is still underrepresented in Ottawa. Meech became a symbol of regional grievances that exist quite independent of the Accord. For Canadians who believe they will never be dealt with fairly by Ottawa, Meech Lake is perceived as one more unfair surrender to the province of Quebec.

Quebec, too, has changed. Its political and business élites say openly that the rest of Canada constitutes an impediment. "Maîtres chez nous" is no longer a manifestation of introspective, insecure parochialism, but of aggressive, expansionary confidence. If the other provinces want to play the game, they must accept Quebec's rules. If not, Quebec is prepared to pick up its ball and go home. The overwhelming support for free trade in Quebec in the mid-1980s was emblematic of its emerging optimism about its ability to stand alone.

The other regions of Canada will experience their own identity crises in the years ahead. Despite their dreams of oil-based wealth, the Atlantic Provinces have been forced to confront their dependence on Ottawa. The closing of the Summerside airbase, the decline of the East Coast fishery, the protracted wrangle over the Hibernia oil fields off Newfoundland – all are symptoms of acute alienation. Even Ontario, which has always had the strongest sense of national identity – and has always confused the national interest with its own – is suffering from self-doubt as it comes to terms with economic stresses it hardly knew existed.

In the past, Canadians paid nothing for their bickering, but Meech Lake has raised the stakes. English Canadians think the French are bluffing when they threaten separation. However, the demise of the Accord has generated renewed separatist pressures, and this may moderate anglophone views. If the failure of the Accord threatens the country they cherish as the best in the world, English Canadians may become more accommodating.

Beyond Meech Lake, Canadian attitudes in the 1990s will be shaped by the impact of free trade with the United States. There were doubts about the agreement at the end of the 1980s, and they may grow as more Canadians become aware of global developments. We have always been at best ambivalent about the United States. Now, with the Japanese and European economies threatening to overtake America's, we may decide that we tied our future prosperity to the wrong partner. Or we might conclude that we are stuck with the Americans whether we like it or not, and can no longer find solace in what one Canadian historian called "the narcissism of small differences." We share the continent. Common markets are the wave of the future. Perhaps it's time to get together and make the best of free trade. The other option – isolation and economic decline – is simply unthinkable.

FACTS

Percentage of theatrical time in Canada devoted to Canadian films in the 1980s: 3

Percentage of video film cassettes that are Canadian: 2-4

Percentage of prime-time, English-language drama that is Canadian: 5

Percentage of magazines sold that are Canadian: 23

Percentage of record and tape sales that are Canadian: 15

THE SUM OF THE PARTS

CHAPTER 2

"The father of confederation is deadlock."

GOLDWIN SMITH

"Whatever you do, adhere to the Union. We are a great country and shall become one of the greatest in the universe if we preserve it; we shall sink into insignificance and adversity if we suffer it to be broken."

SIR JOHN A. MACDONALD, 1861

"We believe that we can get along better without Canada than Canada can without us."

RENÉ LÉVESQUE, 1964

THE CONSTITUTIONAL CONFLICT THAT CONSUMED CANADA IN the final years of the 1980s and the first six months of 1990 sprang organically from events that shaped regional thinking through the decade. In Atlantic Canada, the collapse of oil prices, and the consequent delay in offshore resource developments, deferred again the century-old desire to escape the crippling dependence on the federal government. That bitter disappointment was followed by what seemed like politically motivated punishment, after three Atlantic provinces rejected Conservative governments in favour of Liberals: the cancellation of the nuclear-submarine program, the cutbacks at Via Rail, the closing of the air-force base in Summerside, P.E.I., the threat posed by the parliamentary debate over unemployment insurance, the perilous state of the quota-restricted fishery, and the lingering uncertainty over the Hibernia

WHAT DOES ENGLISH CANADA REALLY WANT   This was the question that troubled Quebec Premier Robert Bourassa in the eleventh-hour negotiations that preceded the demise of the Meech Lake Accord in June 1990.

"Resolving the issue of Quebec's signature on the Constitution was one of the reasons I went into public life....But because it was such a delicate matter, it had to be carried out with the greatest care. Canada could not afford another constitutional failure."

PRIME MINISTER BRIAN MULRONEY, AFTER THE FIRST MINISTERS SIGNED THE MEECH LAKE ACCORD, JUNE 1987

"Resolving the issue of Quebec's signature on the Constitution was one of the reasons I went into public life....But because it was such a delicate matter, it had to be carried out with the greatest care. Canada could not afford another constitutional failure."

PRIME MINISTER BRIAN MULRONEY, AFTER THE FIRST MINISTERS SIGNED THE MEECH LAKE ACCORD, JUNE 1987

"This is a sad day for Canada."

PRIME MINISTER BRIAN MULRONEY, ON THE DEATH OF THE MEECH LAKE ACCORD, JUNE 1990

oil development. In this context, it was a marvel that Newfoundland Premier Clyde Wells did not have more support for his anti-Meech Lake position from his Atlantic Canada colleagues.

But the real marvel was Quebec: it emerged from its 1980 referendum on sovereignty-association more secure than ever about its language and culture, and determined to play a larger, more aggressive role in the Canadian federation. What followed amounted to a second Quiet Revolution. No longer were Quebeckers reflexively looking inward; instead, led by the country's boldest entrepreneurs, the province signalled to the rest of the country that it was willing to play by the rules of the game – confident it could win. The best evidence was free trade, the highest levels of support for which were registered in Quebec. In effect, the nationalists had graduated from the cafés and theatres into the boardrooms. It was that psychological transformation, so little understood in English Canada, that set the stage for Premier Robert Bourassa's five minimum demands for accepting the 1982 constitution.

Ontario, as always, continued to confuse its own interests with those of the rest of Canada, never seeing a contradiction – a political astigmatism that would ultimately distort the constitutional debate. In the meantime, the prosperous boom years of 1985-89 simply confirmed what Ontario had long assumed: that it was the lead engine of the Canadian economy and should enjoy the fruits of that leadership in growth, employment, and income. The formation of David Peterson's Liberal government in 1985 and its electoral victory in 1987 contained no implicit indictment of the Conservative régime, which had ruled Ontario for 42 years. It was instead an evolutionary change: a vote for modernity – for a future Ontarians assumed would be not unlike the past. But having soared to great economic heights, Ontario seemed poised for a great fall. In what had been the bullish epicentre of power and influence, the end of the decade brought concern about the negative side effects of progress.

For Western Canada, the constitutional impasse of 1990 was the logical extension of a long decade's worth of political grievances – from Pierre Trudeau's "Why should I sell your wheat?" to the Liberal government's revenue-grabbing National Energy Program. The election of Brian Mulroney's Conservatives in 1984 briefly persuaded Westerners that, with the likes of Joe Clark and Don

Mazankowski in cabinet, the West would finally get its due. But the illusion was shattered: when the economic recovery arrived, it arrived principally in Central Canada. And the Bank of Canada's tight-money, high-interest-rate policies of the late 1980s were designed to choke an inflationary dragon that, until 1990, barely existed west of Ontario. The inescapable conclusion of Western Canadians was that the political hue of government, Liberal or Conservative, did not matter: Ontario and Quebec would always find a way to leave the West with the short end of the economic stick. The West's demand for Senate reform symbolized its view of itself as the victim of political castration. In opinion polls, this sentiment was nowhere stronger than in Manitoba.

As the decade began, Canadians recognized the importance of the constitutional debate. In September 1980, before the constitutional conference of first ministers, 77% of respondents said the outcome of the talks would have some impact on their personal lives; and 92% believed the discussions would affect the country as a whole. There was widespread support (71%) for Prime Minister Pierre Trudeau's objective: to patriate the Constitution from Great Britain. Significantly, however, only 46% supported such action in the absence of a federal-provincial agreement on how to amend the document; Canadians did not want Ottawa to act unilaterally. By December 1980, after the collapse of talks between the prime minister and the ten provincial premiers, only 27% favoured unilateral measures to patriate the Constitution. (In Alberta, the figure was just 16%.) In fact, a majority said Great Britain should not endorse Ottawa's constitutional package until the Canadian courts had ruled on the legal challenge mounted by the provinces.

What troubled Canadians was the open wound of federal-provincial relations. Most people viewed it as debilitating to the country, and most blamed the federal government. In the spring of 1981, only 21% thought Ottawa had done a good job on federal-provincial relations; approval ratings for the provinces were much higher, ranging from 25% for Quebec to 55% in Ontario. Canadians felt that unilateral action on the Constitution would only aggravate political tensions.

Support for federal unilateralism continued to decline, although the debate was supplanted to some extent by other constitutional issues – the amending formula and the attempt to

FACTS

Percentage of Canada's population represented by Inuit and Indian groups: 2

Number of native Indians, Métis and Inuit in Canada in 1986: 711,725
Estimated number of Indians in 1989: 548,945
Number of Métis: 151,605
Number of Inuit: 36,460
Province with the highest percentage of total native population: Ontario (23.5)

"It would mean constitutional stagnation for Canada for all time."

THE HON. JOHN VALENTINE CLYNE, A FORMER JUDGE OF THE B.C. SUPREME COURT, ON THE TRUDEAU GOVERN-MENT'S PROPOSAL TO GIVE ONTARIO AND QUEBEC VETOS OVER FUTURE AMENDMENTS, NOVEMBER 1980

entrench a Charter of Rights. About 42% supported the inclusion of such a charter, compared with 35% who were opposed. But 22% voiced no opinion, testimony to a large degree of uncertainty about what the Charter was and why it was important. And despite the general support, some 45% said they would be likelier to support the constitutional package if the Charter of Rights were omitted and renegotiated with the provinces – further evidence of Canadian desires to seek resolution rather than fuel discord.

Even the Supreme Court of Canada's September 1981 decision, which dismissed the provincial challenge and declared the federal constitutional proposals legal, did not radically change public opinion on unilateralism. If anything, it hardened attitudes on both sides. (Opposition to unilateral action was strongest in the Western provinces and among francophones in Quebec; support was most evident among Ontarians and, curiously, francophones living outside Quebec.) Canadians continued to blame Ottawa for the ugly state of federal-provincial relations and, as a result, were unwilling to endorse a package that lacked provincial consent. Indeed, 50% said – just before the Supreme Court ruling – that the provinces should continue to challenge Ottawa even if the high court were to rule in favour of the federal government.

Western antagonism towards Ottawa was also evident in surveys on electoral and Senate reform. In the autumn of 1981, 65% of respondents – 71% on the prairies – said they favoured changes that would improve regional representation. Senate reform was equally popular, with 60% saying senators should be elected; only 11% suggested keeping the current system of federal appointment.

By December 1981, Trudeau and the premiers – except Quebec's René Lévesque – had found an acceptable compromise for patriating the Constitution and including a Charter of Rights and Freedoms. Most Canadians (54%) endorsed the agreement, saying it would have a positive effect on the country. The rationale was uncomplicated: most people thought Canada should have its own constitution and most felt patriation would improve national unity. Still, a significant minority – one in three – voiced the opposite view: any agreement excluding Quebec would damage Canadian unity and strain relations on the so-called Quebec issue. Negative attitudes were predictably strongest in Quebec itself (45%).

THE CONSTITUTION: TEN YEARS OF TURMOIL

Feb. 1980: Quebec's National Assembly approves wording of a referendum on sovereignty-association.

Feb. 1980: Pierre Trudeau leads the federal Liberal Party to re-election over Joe Clark's Conservatives.

May 1980: Quebeckers reject by 60-40 the sovereignty-association referendum.

June 1980: Ottawa begins constitutional talks with the provinces. The talks break off in August without agreement on constitutional change.

Sept. 1980: Constitutional talks resume between the federal and provincial governments and end again without agreement.

Oct. 1980: Debate begins in the House of Commons on the Liberal government's motion to patriate the Constitution and add a Charter of Rights and Freedoms.

Oct. 1980: Eight provinces (Ontario and New Brunswick not included) challenge the legality of Ottawa's constitutional proposal.

Jan. 1981: Justice Minister Jean Chrétien redrafts the Charter of Rights, ceding more powers to the provinces and to native Canadians.

Feb. 1981: Manitoba's Court of Appeal rules the constitutional package and amendments legally valid.

March 1981: The Progressive Conservatives mount a filibuster in the Commons during final debate on the constitutional package.

April 1981: Quebec's Court of Appeal rules in favour of the constitutional package.

April 1981: Except for Quebec and Ontario, the provinces agree that the Constitution be patriated without revision and suggest a new amending formula. Ottawa declines to accept the provincial proposal.

Sept. 1981: The Supreme Court of Canada finds the federal constitutional proposal legal but suggests that Ottawa not act unilaterally.

FACTS

In 1986, some 415,898 natives were classified as status Indians, belonging to one of 595 different Indian bands and living on 2,277 reserves, situated on 2.6 million hectares of land. Newfoundland was the only province in 1981 without a resident Indian band. Almost two-thirds of all Inuit live in the Northwest Territories, the remainder in the Yukon, Arctic Quebec, Labrador, and northern Ontario.

"I'd like the right to be understood as well as to speak."

LARRY DESJARDINS, A MANITOBA MLA, AFTER WINNING THE RIGHT TO SPEAK FRENCH IN THE PROVINCIAL LEGISLATURE ONLY TO FIND THAT HANSARD PUBLISHED ONLY THE FRENCH VERSION OF HIS REMARKS, 1981

Nov. 1981: The prime minister and all the provinces except Quebec agree to patriate the Constitution, on a formula for amending the document (the agreement of seven provinces and 50% of the population), and on the creation of a two-tiered Charter of Rights.

Dec. 1981: The House of Commons votes 246-24 to patriate the Constitution with the agreed-upon amending formula and the Charter of Rights and Freedoms. The Senate, by a vote of 59-23, lends its support a few days later.

March 1982: Queen Elizabeth II proclaims the Constitution Act. Quebec Premier René Lévesque boycotts the ceremony.

June 1983: Brian Mulroney defeats former Prime Minister Joe Clark for the leadership of the Progressive Conservative party.

Feb. 1984: Pierre Trudeau announces his resignation as leader of the Liberal Party.

June 1984: John Turner defeats Jean Chrétien to win the leadership of the Liberal party. He is prime minister of Canada for 79 days.

Sept. 1984: Conservative Brian Mulroney wins the federal election.

Dec. 1985: Liberal Robert Bourassa defeats the Parti Québécois's Pierre-Marc Johnson to become Premier of Quebec.

June 1985: The Conservative minority government of Ontario resigns and is replaced by the Liberals under David Peterson.

April 1987: Prime Minister Mulroney and the ten provincial premiers meet at Meech Lake in the Gatineau Hills outside Ottawa. During ten hours of discussion, the first draft of what will become the Meech Lake Accord is hammered out.

June 1987: Meeting in the Langevin Block on Wellington Street in Ottawa, the prime minister and the ten provincial premiers agree on the legal wording of the Meech Lake constitutional accord.

June 1987: Quebec becomes the first province to ratify the Meech Lake Accord, setting in motion a three-year constitutional clock that requires all the other provinces to give their consent by June 23, 1990.

Oct. 1987: The House of Commons ratifies the Meech Lake Accord. The amendments would: allow the provinces to veto changes in the structure or power of the House of Commons, the Senate, or the Supreme Court; require unanimous consent of the ten provinces for creation of any new province; require the federal government to choose nominees to the Senate and the Supreme Court from lists of names submitted by the provinces; recognize Quebec as a distinct society; permit the provinces to opt out of shared-cost programs in areas of provincial jurisdiction, using federal funds to create their own programs; and permit the provinces to control immigration.

Oct. 1987: Frank McKenna leads the New Brunswick Liberal party into power, winning all seats in the legislature, and succeeding Conservative Richard Hatfield, who ruled the province for 17 years.

April 1988: The Senate sends the Meech Lake document back to the Commons with extensive amendments.

April 1988: Conservative Gary Filmon is elected premier of Manitoba, with a minority government, complicating the search for political consensus on the constitutional question.

June 1988: The House of Commons votes 200 to 7 to override the Senate's proposed amendments to Meech Lake.

Nov. 1988: Brian Mulroney leads the Conservative party to victory in the federal election.

Dec. 1988: The Supreme Court of Canada strikes down part of Quebec's language laws, ruling that French-only signs and advertisements constitute an unreasonable restriction on free speech guarantees in the Canadian Charter of Rights and Freedoms. The same month, Quebec invokes the "notwithstanding" clause in the Charter to override the guarantee. The law is approved by the National Assembly with only modest amendments.

April 1989: Clyde Wells, a constitutional lawyer, leads the Newfoundland Liberal party into government, ending 17 years of Conservative rule in the province. The election will have profound consequences for the Meech Lake Accord.

FACTS

The interests of status Indians are represented by the Assembly of First Nations; those of the Inuit are represented by the Inuit Tapirisat of Canada; and those of the Métis and non-status Indians by the Métis National Council and the Native Council of Canada.

41

"No matter what the opinion of the court, this project will continue to be perfectly illegitimate, politically unjustifiable and even immoral."

RENÉ LÉVESQUE, AWAITING THE DECISION OF THE SUPREME COURT OF CANADA ON THE FEDERAL GOVERNMENT'S CONSTITUTIONAL PACKAGE, 1981

Oct. 1989: Stan Waters, a member of the Reform Party, wins an election in Alberta to be that province's nominee to the Senate. After initially refusing to seat him, the Mulroney government reverses course in June 1990.

June 1990: Brian Mulroney and the ten provincial premiers meet in closed session in Ottawa, seeking to resolve the Meech Lake impasse. After a week, they emerge with an apparent compromise. But the understanding quickly breaks down. In Manitoba, native MLA Elijah Harper forces the legislature to adjourn before public hearings on the Accord can be held. In Newfoundland, Premier Clyde Wells adjourns the House of Assembly, rather than put the Accord to a vote. In Ottawa, federal officials announce that Meech Lake is officially dead.

July 1990: Quebec announces that it will establish a commission to discuss proposals for its future for presentation to Ottawa in 1991.

ODD MAN OUT   The Meech Lake Accord's most outspoken critic, and in the end the only premier who opposed it, Clyde Wells of Newfoundland spoke for many English Canadians – and 75 percent of Newfoundlanders.

In April 1982, Queen Elizabeth II proclaimed the Constitution Act, removing the final vestige of British authority in Canada. For several years thereafter, despite on-going discussions between Ottawa and the provinces, constitutional issues receded from public attention. Still, in one 1986 survey, majorities of respondents agreed that it was important for Quebec to sign the constitutional agreement (69%) and supported recognizing Quebec as a distinct society (55%) in order to win that signature. Then, in June 1987, Prime Minister Brian Mulroney and the ten provincial premiers reached agreement in principle on a series of amendments that became known as the Meech Lake Accord, the basic thrust of which was to embrace Quebec within the Constitution.

One criticism that would plague the Accord for the next three years was evident almost immediately – the surrender of federal powers to the provinces. Although 50% said the agreement was worth the cost, almost as many (45%) maintained that Ottawa had paid too high a price, one that would ultimately weaken national programs. Most Canadians continued to cite the importance of Quebec's accepting the Constitution – 69% in the summer of 1988; the numbers were even higher among francophones outside and anglophones inside Quebec. But only 47% said they favoured recognizing Quebec as a distinct society in Canada (an 8% drop in two years), compared with 51% that opposed granting such recognition. In fact, declines in support for distinct-society status were recorded in every province but two – Prince Edward Island and Quebec itself. Opposition was especially notable in the West, particularly Manitoba (73%). Not surprisingly, those who supported recognizing Quebec as a unique entity within Canada were most likely to endorse the Meech Lake Accord; and those against granting Quebec distinct-society status were most likely to oppose the agreement.

The absence of constitutional consensus was also reflected in attitudes towards bilingualism. In July 1988, several Western Tory backbenchers defied party discipline and voted against Bill C-72, which amended the Official Languages Act to augment bilingual services in the federal government. Earlier, Saskatchewan had repealed a law requiring that all legislation be translated into French; a $60-million federal grant was needed to change the province's mind. And Alberta introduced a bill to allow French in

FACTS

Amount Ottawa spent on health services for native people in 1987: $417 million

The reliability and accuracy of data used to evaluate its program, according to Auditor-General Kenneth Dye: questionable

Average age of death for Canada's status Indians of both sexes in 1976: 44

"Quebec's argument conjures up a picture of a totalitarian conception of society to which the court cannot adhere."

JULES DESCHENES, CHIEF JUSTICE OF THE QUEBEC SUPERIOR COURT, IN RULING THAT THE CANADIAN CHARTER OF RIGHTS AND FREEDOMS TOOK PRECEDENCE OVER QUEBEC'S BILL 101, THE 1977 LAW THAT ATTEMPTED TO BAN ANGLOPHONES FROM ATTENDING ENGLISH SCHOOLS IN THE PROVINCE, 1982

the courts and the legislature, but made no provision for translating laws into French and declined federal funds to do so. Anti-French sentiments were further aroused in December of 1988, with the passage of Quebec's Bill 178, requiring the use of the French language only on outdoor commercial signs; some 76% voiced opposition to the bill, and most respondents believed it would complicate passage of the Meech Lake Accord. It is possible that firm action by Ottawa to invalidate Bill 178 might have appeased Westerners and helped to save the Accord. But without such action, the West regarded Bill 178 as yet another instance of unfairness.

Doubts about Meech's success continued to grow through the spring of 1989. By the summer, with two provinces still withholding formal ratification (Manitoba and New Brunswick), 70% were predicting it would not be approved. The percentage was even higher in Manitoba (79%). Moreover, fully 50% of those who forecast the demise of the Meech Accord said its failure would be good for Canada. One year before the Accord's ultimate collapse, Canadians were deeply skeptical about its chances and deeply divided about the consequences for the country. Inevitably, these attitudes hardened political resolve in the hold-out provinces.

In fact, by the autumn of 1989 the opposition to the Meech Lake amendments looked increasingly formidable. Newfoundland Premier Clyde Wells was openly threatening to revoke the province's ratification. Manitoba had tabled an all-party report demanding 12 additional amendments – the direct result of anger over Bill 178. And New Brunswick had published a similar, albeit more accommodating document. Decima survey results reflected this stiffening resistance. Between June 1988 and September 1989, support for the pact dropped from 54% to 35%; opposition increased from 41% to 51%. And the "no opinion" category doubled, from 7% to 14%, indicating growing confusion about its merits. The September 1989 results also revealed how polarized Canadians had become. In Manitoba, only 12% of respondents said they favoured the Accord; in Quebec, 52% did.

Remarkably, two out of three people continued to say it was important that Quebec accept the Constitution. They were simply not prepared to meet Robert Bourassa's basic demands. The chief sticking point seemed to be the distinct society. An outright majority (55%) opposed granting Quebec that status within

SUPPORT FOR THE MEECH LAKE ACCORD

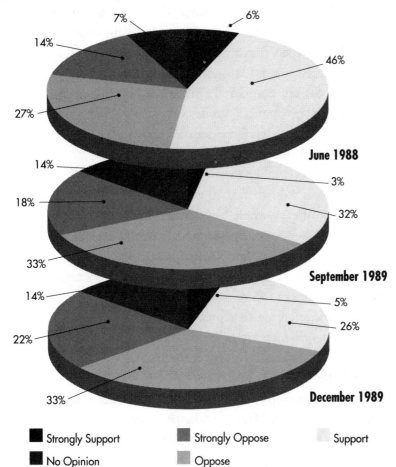

7%
6%
14%
46%
27%
June 1988

14%
3%
18%
32%
33%
September 1989

14%
5%
22%
26%
33%
December 1989

■ Strongly Support   ■ Strongly Oppose   □ Support
■ No Opinion   ▨ Oppose

FACTS

Number of houses on the Piapot Indian Reserve near Regina in 1980: 11
Number that had running water and toilets: 4

THE PROBLEM WITH MEECH LAKE

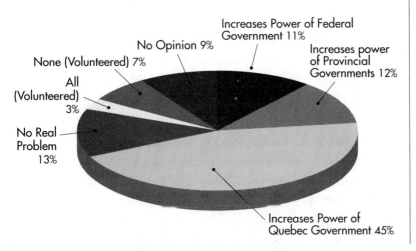

Increases Power of Federal Government 11%
No Opinion 9%
None (Volunteered) 7%
Increases power of Provincial Governments 12%
All (Volunteered) 3%
No Real Problem 13%
Increases Power of Quebec Government 45%

"I have never seen an issue so often buried that is still discussed by so many people so vehemently."

JACQUES PARIZEAU, CONTEMPLATING THE SUBJECT OF QUEBEC SEPARATISM DURING HIS BID FOR THE LEADERSHIP OF THE PARTI QUÉBÉCOIS, 1987

the Constitution. The percentages were even higher in Western Canada. The population was sharply divided on two other Meech-related questions as well: 49% agreed with the statement "I am tired of giving special treatment to francophones in Quebec," but 42% disagreed. And 43% said it didn't matter whether Meech Lake was passed, compared with 39% that said it did. Again, however, the "no opinion" group was extraordinarily high (18%), another indication that Canadians did not understand the importance of the Meech amendments.

Support continued to ebb into the winter of 1989 – down to 31% in December. In fact, the anti-Meech forces were gaining ground almost everywhere but Quebec, where 52% still endorsed the Accord. Elsewhere, opposition had climbed to 69% in Manitoba and 75% in Newfoundland. And when Canadians were asked to cite the primary problem with the Meech Lake document, by far the largest number (45%) pointed at Quebec, saying the amendments would increase that province's power; only 12% said the problem was an increase in provincial-government power generally. Nor did Canadians fear Meech's collapse: 60% said the failure to ratify the Accord would make no substantial difference to the future of the country; only 32% thought failure would increase regional tensions and tear the country apart.

But it was clear as we entered the new decade that the bitterness of the Meech Lake debate had already left its mark. In 1983, two of three respondents had disagreed with the suggestion that English be Canada's only official language. By March of 1990, 42% said bilingualism was a source of constant conflict and that we'd be better off with just one official language. A large minority (39%) also said it supported measures passed by several Ontario towns and cities in 1989 declaring them English-only communities. The link between bilingualism and Meech Lake was also clear. Among proponents of unilingualism, opposition to Meech Lake was decidedly stronger.

Asked to state their principal reason for opposing the Meech amendments, most respondents cited factors involving Quebec. Twenty-three percent said Meech conferred preferential status on Quebec; 11% pointed to the distinct-society clause; 4% indicated bilingualism. By the end, almost no-one mentioned issues that had also generated criticism of the Accord: the dilution of federal

THE UNILINGUAL DEBATE

Would you support the adoption of an English-only or French-only law in your community?

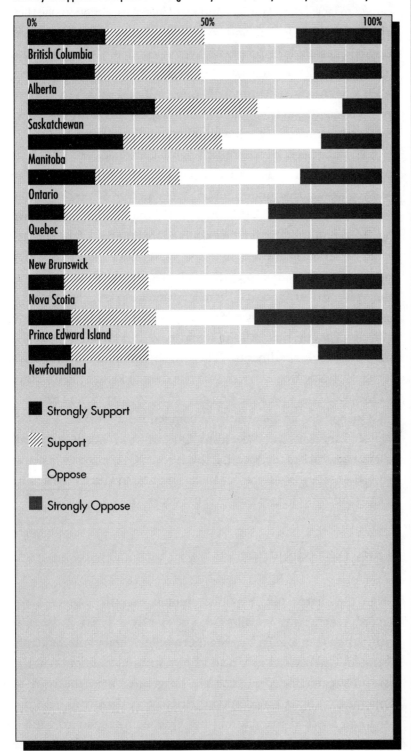

0%		50%	100%
British Columbia			
Alberta			
Saskatchewan			
Manitoba			
Ontario			
Quebec			
New Brunswick			
Nova Scotia			
Prince Edward Island			
Newfoundland			

◼ Strongly Support

▨ Support

☐ Oppose

◼ Strongly Oppose

FACTS

Year when gasoline sniffing was first identified as a problem on Manitoba Indian reserves: 1973
Number of Indian children estimated to be addicted to gasoline fumes in northern Manitoba in 1987: 1,380
Amount Ottawa spent fighting drug abuse on Manitoba Indian reserves in 1982: $500,000
Amount spent in 1987: $2.5 million

"I am biting my fingernails as to the long-term implications of the concessions made to the provinces. This deal marks a major decentralization of power within an already decentralized state."

STEPHEN SCOTT, PROFESSOR OF CONSTITUTIONAL LAW AT McGILL UNIVERSITY, ASSESSING THE MEECH LAKE ACCORD, 1987

power or the changing nature of Senate appointments. Even as the Meech Lake drama moved towards its dénouement, Canadians seemed to lack a broad understanding of its terms. Emotionally, they were fixated on Quebec and sharply divided along linguistic and regional lines. Perhaps prophetically, 56% said in March 1990 that the Accord contained too many problems and should not be passed, "even if it means constitutional issues will plague us for years to come." Only one in three thought ratifying the amendments would allow the country to "get on with other important issues."

Looking back, it is clear that English Canadians simply did not grasp the profound changes that had occurred in Quebec in the 1980s. Lacking that understanding, they perceived no risk to the nation if Meech Lake failed. They doubted that Quebec would leave Confederation and, if it did, they doubted that the rest of the country would be seriously affected. With no appreciation of the risk, they had no reason to agree to Quebec's terms. The situation was precisely reversed in Quebec. From its vantage point, its economic maturity entitled it to play a leadership role in Canada and to have custody of its destiny. And it would have it with or without the Meech Lake amendments. The whole rationale of Quebec's demands sprang from its desire to seize the economic infrastructure of Quebec Inc. – to preserve French culture by growing and expanding. Quebec had an agenda: to be competitive in world markets. If English Canadians had other ideas, Quebec wasn't about to mourn. Now, in the wake of the Meech Lake debacle, Quebeckers will determine where they fit – if they fit at all – in the Canadian mosaic. The rest of Canada will have no say in the decision.

INTO THE NINETIES

Given the sharp split in public opinion over the Meech Lake Accord, reactions to its failure will be starkly different in English and French Canada. In Quebec there will be jubilation. Suddenly liberated, Quebec can now plan its own future, confident that the risks of greater independence are no greater than the risks of remaining within Confederation. Elsewhere, there will be a belated and shocked recognition that Quebec has changed fundamentally, concern (at last) about the consequences of letting the

SHOULD QUEBEC SIGN?

How important is it that Quebec
sign the Canadian constitution?

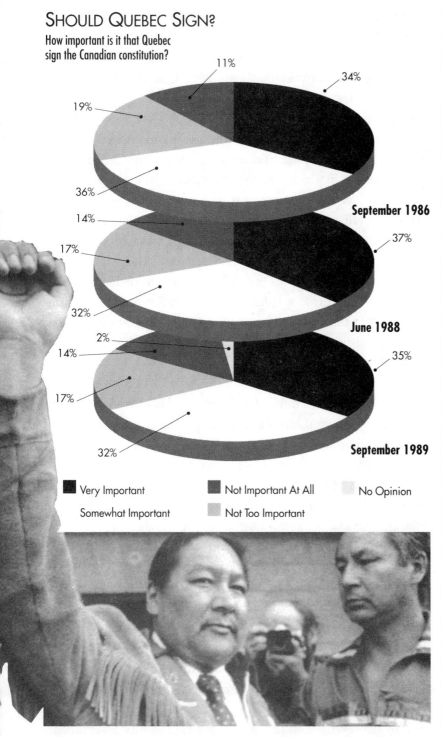

11%

34%

19%

36%

14%

September 1986

17%

37%

32%

June 1988

2%

14%

35%

17%

32%

September 1989

■ Very Important   ■ Not Important At All   No Opinion

Somewhat Important   Not Too Important

NATIVE POWER   Largely ignored in the decade-long debate over the constitution, growing aboriginal resentment – articulated by Elijah Harper,
an emboldened Manitoba MLA – helped scuttle the Meech Lake Accord.

"By leaving without an agreement, we are signing a blank cheque for those who want to oppress us."

JIM SINCLAIR, SPOKESMAN FOR CANADA'S MÉTIS GROUPS, AFTER THE COLLAPSE OF TALKS WITH FIRST MINISTERS TO ENTRENCH NATIVE SELF-GOVERNMENT IN THE CONSTITUTION, 1987

Meech amendments die, and questions about whether anything can still be done to save the nation.

That will be Act One. In Act Two, an angry English Canada will indulge in recriminations, accusing Quebec of tearing the country apart. In French Canada, sober second thoughts will stir doubts about whether complete independence is a good idea after all, at least economically, and whether it might not be more prudent to slow the pace of disentanglement from Canada. That is the direction in which Premier Bourassa is guiding Quebeckers.

Whatever the outcome, it is now evident that we will never have a federalism like the one that existed before June 23, 1990 – that some new form of constitutional arrangement, probably close to sovereignty-association, must be achieved. But with English Canadians embittered by Quebec's approach to de facto separation, the actual divorce is likely to be complicated and acrimonious, rather than civil and painless. There will be voices calling for calm, dispassionate negotiations, but once the lawyers are involved it may turn nasty.

The political consequences of the Accord's demise are frightening. It is unlikely that Jean Chrétien, given his anti-Meech position, will win more than a handful of seats in Quebec in the next election. The question is whether Brian Mulroney can win any seats outside Quebec. By 1993, Canada may resemble Italy, a country whose post-war politics have been a synonym for stalemate. In the next election, the Liberals may win 30 seats in Atlantic Canada; the Tories might win five. In Quebec, where the Conservative machine will continue political handouts to shore up support, Mulroney may emerge with 70 seats; Chrétien might win five. Ontario is more difficult to predict, but 50 seats for the Liberals, 30 for the Tories, and 20 for the New Democrats does not seem improbable. (Several of those seats may be decided by candidates' positions on abortion, which remains one of the country's most inflammatory issues.) The West will be more divided, with the three established parties and the Reform Party of Canada each winning about 25 seats.

In that event, Canada would have no majority government, no party truly representing the national interest, and no hope of progress on the constitutional front. Aboriginal rights, Senate reform, more political power for the Yukon and Northwest

Territories: these problems would await a new generation of political leadership. An impasse on native issues would be particularly troubling: the violent confrontation between Quebec police and Mohawk Indians in Oka in July 1990 suggests that Indian frustration could become explosive.

Could a pro-Quebec Mulroney forge any sort of alliance with the anti-Meech Reform Party? Highly unlikely. Could Chrétien? Perhaps, but only at the cost of more political damage in Quebec. As a result, the New Democrats, the country's most irrelevant political entity through the previous decade, might well inherit a balance of power.

Had Meech Lake passed, Brian Mulroney might not have sought a third term. His mark in the history books would have been made. But Mulroney harbours deep feelings about Quebec and is intensely competitive. The prospect of his withdrawing from a campaign almost certain to be fought on the future of the country is remote. Whether he can win again is another question. Many Quebeckers will ask why they should support Mulroney – or participate at all – since the new Quebec will have so much less to do with the federal government. That same problem will confront any federal leader trying to accommodate a province that has already decided Ottawa doesn't speak for Quebec. Jean Chrétien is personable, but his credibility – especially in the West – rests on his ability to sell the federalist position to Quebeckers. With the failure of Meech Lake, that talent is diminished. If the next election turns on the issue of who can strike the sanest deal with Quebec, Mulroney – despite his current standing in the polls – might well win. What makes the situation all the more absurd is that the Liberal party is led by a French Canadian who has credibility only in English Canada, while the Conservatives are led by an Irish Canadian who depends on his Quebec base for mere survival.

In the meantime, the federal government must await Quebec's demands, a process that will take us into 1991. Ottawa can be expected to recognize political reality. It will attempt to strike the most reasonable deal it can with Quebec, ceding sovereignty in such areas as immigration and telecommunications. But the real debate, the debate about Quebec's future, will be held exclusively within its own borders. English Canada will not even be consulted.

FACTS

The population of Iqaluit, Northwest Territories: 2,500
Estimated number of Iqaluit Indian women who report assaults per month: 50

Percentage of Secretary of State's budget allocated to native programs in 1989: 2
Percentage of cuts in that ministry's budget allocated to native programs: 44

WHO DO YOU LOVE?

CHAPTER 3

"Love all, trust a few."
WILLIAM SHAKESPEARE, ALL'S WELL THAT ENDS WELL, 1601-03

"Put not your trust in princes."

PSALMS, CXLVI.3

GOVERNMENTS SAID ONE THING, THEN DID ANOTHER. POLITICIANS lied, stole, and abused the system. Business leaders, obsessed with private profit, neglected the public interest. Teachers transformed themselves into unionists, more concerned about contracts than about students. Clergy of various churches preached virtue and practised vice. Labour unions flirted with obsolescence. Is it any wonder that the institutions dominating Canadian life in the 1980s lost public confidence?

The 1980s demonstrated all too clearly that the rules that once governed society no longer worked; anyone who continued to play by those rules was therefore a steward of the status quo – and automatically suspect. Paradoxically, discarding the old rules conferred a sense of independence and power on Canadians. They refused, a priori, to believe what traditional authorities said, confident that they could make up their own minds. Politicians, businessmen, priests, and rabbis who claimed to have solutions for problems threw themselves utterly out of sync with a population that knew instinctively that solutions had not yet been devised.

In politics, at least, the system itself was partly to blame. Canadians set very high standards for public office, perhaps too

A MATTER OF TRUST   The resignation of Conservative minister Sinclair Stevens amid charges of conflict of interest in 1986 was only one of a series of government scandals that eroded public confidence in politicians.

"It could have happened in any Ontario town. There's nothing particularly bad about Prescott."

STEPHEN HEDER, DIRECTOR OF THE FAMILY AND CHILDREN'S SERVICE OF LEEDS-GRENVILLE, AFTER 32 CHARGES OF SEXUAL ABUSE OF YOUNG BOYS ARE LAID AGAINST FOUR MEN AND TWO YOUTHS, 1989

high. Those who might meet those standards are deterred by the prospect of such close scrutiny. And those who have never run afoul of social propriety, if not the law – who have never smoked marijuana, told an ethnic joke, or failed to pay a parking ticket – no longer exist in significant numbers. Too often, the men and women who are attracted to politics tend to be those who think they can manipulate the system for their own benefit. Not surprisingly, 85% of Canadians say they would never consider running for public office.

The collapse of confidence in government was apparent in Decima surveys throughout the decade. Between June 1987 and September 1989, the percentage of respondents who said that our "system of government" is one thing that makes Canada the best place in the world to live dropped from 70 to 62. Similarly, no fewer than 75% agreed that governments tend to pay more attention to the interests of big business than to those of the common man. And almost half said that none of Canada's political parties "really stand for the things I believe in," a shocking indictment.

Politicians enjoy even less trust. In the early 1980s, most Canadians described them as hardworking (70%), principled (63%), and competent (57%). And 51% said they held somewhat (or very) favourable feelings toward politicians. But by March 1990, that faith had dramatically eroded. Now, 57% of respondents say politicians are unprincipled; 81% think they are more concerned with making money than with helping people; 65% call them incompetent; and only 32% of the population say they hold generally favourable views about them; 64% say their opinions are unfavourable. (Westerners tend to regard politicians in the most negative light; Quebeckers are the most positive.)

Other surveys confirmed that politics in the 1980s was a profession either for the intrepid or for the insensate. In September 1984, only 45% said politicians could be trusted to do what was best for the country; in December 1988, only 37% did. And two-thirds agreed that "the ethical and moral standards of politicians have really gone down in recent years."

Inevitably, this sentiment translates into mistrust of both federal and provincial governments – and, indeed, the civil service. Net confidence in Ottawa went from zero to a –37 rating in June 1982, doubtless the result of the recession. But it was still at –28 in

March 1989. (The rating is calculated by subtracting the percentage who say they have "hardly any confidence" in the people who run an institution from the percentage who say they have "a great deal" of confidence.) Provincial ratings plunged from +9 in March 1981 to −24 in March 1989. And assessments of civil servants charted a similar course. (Again, the regional split between the sharply critical West and a more supportive Quebec is striking.)

Despite these sentiments, many Canadians think government should continue to play a pivotal role in the nation's economic and social affairs. We want government to erect and maintain a safety net for the disadvantaged, whether they are individuals, industries, or regions. And we would prefer that government not intrude into more personal jurisdictions, where moral or ethical choices are involved. In effect, Canadians want their rulers to walk a fine line: to promote private-sector growth, but protect the public good; to defend individual rights and freedoms, but not at the expense of the broader public interest. At this, most Canadians think government has failed; 45% said in June 1989 that the government was usually more concerned about business than about the public's interests.

Many Canadians have come to view the business world through the same jaundiced eyes. They see Wall Street as a place where the junk-bond trader Michael Milken was allowed to make half a billion dollars a year trading on insider information, confirming Aristotle Onassis's remark that "the secret of business is to know something that nobody else knows." Big business particularly is increasingly regarded not as a creator of wealth – as the Mellons and the Rockefellers once were – but as a harvester of wealth. In the 1980s, entrepreneurial genius was directed largely toward tax avoidance, trying to find ways to circumvent the system. The old paternalistic ethic – that the function of big corporations was to provide jobs and wealth for less-advantaged employees – that, too, did not survive the decade. With the ascendancy of the professional manager, the number one priority became to create wealth for the shareholder, by whatever means.

Our opinions were more sanguine about business than they were about politics; for eight consecutive years (1980-87), four out of five respondents said they held favourable views of business leaders. Still, assessments of their chief characteristics declined

FACTS

In 1988, the first year of tax reform, some 60,000 profitable corporations did not pay tax.
Among them:
Algoma Steel – profits: $80 million
Bramalea – profits: $33 million
Brascade – profits: $64 million
Xerox Canada – profits: $74 million
Tridel Enterprises – profits: $72 million

> "What finance officials did not know was that there were so many dishonest Canadians."

DEPUTY FINANCE MINISTER STANLEY HARTT, COMMENTING ON THE SCIENTIFIC RESEARCH TAX CREDIT PROGRAM, WHICH COST OTTAWA AN ESTIMATED $500 MILLION IN LOST TAX REVENUES

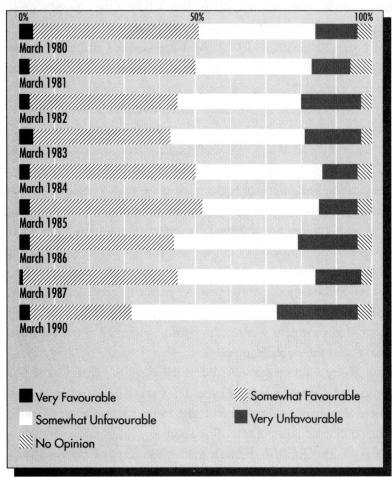

MEASURES OF TRUST - POLITICIANS

How would you describe your feelings toward politicians?

Legend: Very Favourable, Somewhat Favourable, Somewhat Unfavourable, Very Unfavourable, No Opinion

1981 JULY — Six companies, including two Crown corporations, are charged with fixing uranium prices between 1971 and 1978. The Supreme Court of Canada quashes the case against the Crown corporations and charges against the private companies are subsequently dropped.

1982 JAN. — Clifford Olsen, convicted of murdering 11 children in British Columbia, is sentenced to 11 concurrent life terms. A controversy ensues after the RCMP confirms that it paid an Olsen family trust fund $100,000 for information used to locate some of the bodies.

1983 JAN. — The government of Ontario seizes the assets of three trust companies — Greymac, Crown, and Seaway — after a real-estate flip in which the price of 11,000 apartments in Toronto rose from $270 million to $500 million in a matter of weeks.

MEASURES OF TRUST – GOVERNMENT
(Net Ratings*)

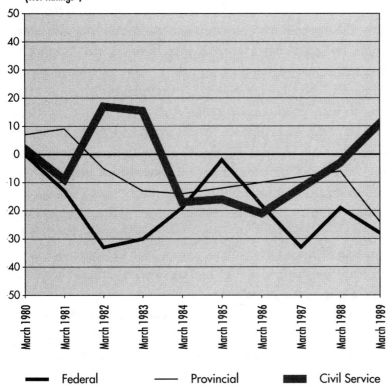

Federal — Provincial — Civil Service

*Net Ratings are calculated by subtracting the percentage who say they have "hardly any confidence" in those who run an institution from the percentage who say they have "a great deal" of confidence.

FACTS

Number of banks, trust and mortgage companies that went out of business in the 1980s: 20

Amount of money the Canada Deposit Insurance Corp. paid out: $4.67 billion

Number that went out of business in the 1970s: 2

Amount paid out by the CDIC: $0

1983 MAY

Micmac Indian Donald Marshall is freed from prison, the first Canadian in history to be convicted of murder and then released after evidence was re-examined.

1983 AUG.

Federal Mines Minister Roger Simmons, in office only 10 days, resigns. Soon after, he is charged with tax evasion. In December 1983 he is convicted and fined $3,500. Simmons remains in the House of Commons until losing his Newfoundland seat in the 1984 election.

1983 NOV.

Amway Corp. is fined $25 million for defrauding Revenue Canada of $28 million in import duties. It is the largest fine ever levied in Canada.

"The time has come when it is totally unacceptable for courts to act as if prison is unthinkable for white-collar defendants, but a matter of routine in other cases. Breaking the law is breaking the law."

JUDGE M. LASKER, SENTENCING CONVICTED INSIDER TRADER IVAN BOESKY, DECEMBER 1989

through the decade. By March 1990, only a slim majority thought business leaders were principled; and 37% said they were incompetent (versus 18% in 1980). Most Canadians agree with the statement that "people who run corporations don't really care about people like me." Most assume that businessmen "cannot be expected to put their country's interest before their own or their company's." And those least likely to trust businessmen are also least likely to trust politicians; in other words, by 1990, a significant segment of the population was disillusioned with both the nation's economic and its political leadership – and the numbers are growing.

Oddly, this absence of faith in business in general is not reflected in attitudes toward the people who run multinational corporations. On Decima's net confidence scale, the multinationals went from –36 in June 1980 to –8 in September 1988. But for most Canadians, small is still more beautiful. In September 1989, small business earned a +41 net confidence rating, one of the highest in ten years of polling.

Our views about specific industries tend to follow the spotlight of news. In the early 1980s, amid fierce debate about Canadian energy policy, net confidence ratings of oil companies dipped as low as –36. With the repeal of the National Energy Program and a drop in oil prices, the evaluation improved, finishing the decade at –10. The forest industry has followed the opposite course, dropping from a +29 ranking in June 1981 to –1 in December 1989. That decline perfectly mirrors assessments of the industry's environmental performance. The ecological factor was even more evident in reviews of the chemical industry; in September 1981, its rating stood at –11; by June 1989, it was –40. Only the tobacco business rates lower. Canadians feel more positively about high-tech companies (+32 in September 1989) and about banks (+4 in June 1989). But confidence in bankers was hurt badly by the recession and by the controversy, later in the decade, over service charges to consumers; in March 1980, the net rating for banks had been +38.

One institution that actually gained lustre in the 1980s was the union movement, although it started the decade at such a low point that it had nowhere to go but up. Unions suffered from a variety of negative opinions. Labour leaders may have been adept at negotiating wage increases, but their members were looking for improvements in non-salary-related areas: a safer and more enjoyable work environment, training programs, daycare facilities. Moreover, the basic function of unions contradicted the values held by most Canadians. The population wanted stability; unions delivered disruption. The population wanted services; unions withdrew them. As the recession deepened, Canadians increasingly felt that organized labour had grown too big and too powerful. To cure the country's economic malaise, more co-operation was needed – among business, labour, and government. Instead, the labour establishment was still preaching the old, discredited policy of confrontation. As with politicians, there was an enormous gap between what union executives were saying and what the rank and file wanted to hear.

So while labour unions began the 1980s at a –30 net confidence rating – among the lowest of the more than forty institutions Decima surveyed – and dropped to –48 in December 1982, they finished the decade at –29. Half of all respondents continued to believe that organized labour was too powerful but, as concerns about social equity grew, many saw a new legitimacy in protecting the interests of average working men and women. Despite the turnaround, the comparative ranking of organized labour remained low. One in three respondents said in December 1989 that unions had outlived their usefulness. As many Canadians thought labour-management relations had deteriorated as thought they had improved (and a majority held labour accountable for the state of those relations). And most people said union leaders were doing an "only fair" (38%) or "poor"(19%) job of meeting the needs of their workers.

Few institutions escaped the pervasive loss of public confidence in the 1980s. The health industry was one. In three consecutive years (1986-88), eight in ten respondents said they held favourable impressions of both doctors and nurses. People offered equally positive assessments of community hospitals. In both categories, older Canadians tended to voice the highest level of confidence. But the highest mark of the decade – a net confidence rating of +45 in the fall of 1989 – went to local police forces. The confidence level rose sharply with age – from +28 among Canadians under twenty to +57 for those over the age of sixty. Ratings were sharply below average in Manitoba, where an inquiry into the police killing of the native leader J.J. Harper was being conducted, and in

FACTS

Number of Canada's 100 largest companies that were widely held in 1986: 20
Number that were widely held in 1990: 12
Percentage of assets of 100 largest corporations that were controlled by widely held public companies in 1990: 23
Value of assets held by the 12: $80.4 billion
Total value of assets of 100 largest corporations: $344.74 billion

"People who come from a business environment, and there are many among Quebec Tories, cannot understand why they should be punished for making money."

LISE BISSONNETTE, ATTEMPTING TO EXPLAIN THE PROPENSITY OF THE QUEBEC CONSERVATIVE MPS FOR RUNNING AFOUL OF CONFLICT-OF-INTEREST GUIDELINES, FEBRUARY 1988

MEASURES OF TRUST - CAPTAINS OF INDUSTRY

How would you describe your feelings toward business leaders?

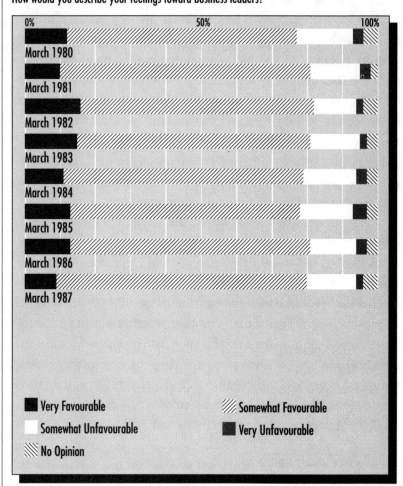

	0%	50%	100%
March 1980			
March 1981			
March 1982			
March 1983			
March 1984			
March 1985			
March 1986			
March 1987			

■ Very Favourable ▨ Somewhat Favourable
□ Somewhat Unfavourable ■ Very Unfavourable
▨ No Opinion

1984 SEPT.

The new Conservative government of Brian Mulroney abolishes the Scientific Research Tax Credit program. Set up by the Liberals in 1984, the program awarded $3.5 billion in tax credits to some 1,900 corporations. Of that amount, only $1.4 billion was allocated to genuine research and development projects.

1985 FEB.

The Minister of Defence, Robert Coates, resigns from cabinet after admitting to visiting a strip club in Lahr, West Germany.

1985 SEPT.

The Minister of Fisheries, John Fraser, is forced to resign from cabinet after admitting that federal inspectors permitted tainted tuna to be shipped and sold in supermarkets.

MEASURES OF TRUST – BUSINESS
(Net Ratings)

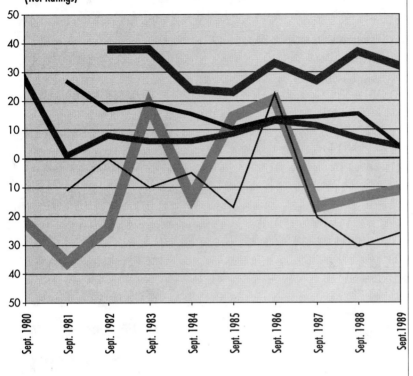

Legend:

- ▬▬ High Tech
- ▬▬ Forest Industry
- ▬▬ Oil Companies
- —— Chemical Industry
- ▬▬ Banks

(Broken line indicates data not available.)

FACTS

Between 1971 and 1981, the number of atheists and agnostics in Canada climbed 70%. In the same decade, Buddhists showed the largest percentage increase of any organized religion: 223%. Pentecostals were up 54%; Mormons, 36%. On the other hand, Unitarians declined in number by 31%, Doukhobors by 27%.

1986 MAY
Federal Minister of Regional Industrial Expansion Sinclair Stevens resigns amid conflict-of-interest allegations. A subsequent judicial inquiry finds Stevens was party to 14 separate conflicts of interest while holding his cabinet portfolio.

1987 JAN.
André Bissonnette, Conservative MP and Minister of State for Transport, resigns from cabinet after charges of conflict of interest in the sale of land in his riding to Oerlikon Aerospace Inc. He was subsequently cleared of fraud charges.

1987 FEB.
Roch LaSalle, a minister of state, resigns from the Mulroney cabinet after allegations that he misused his political power when minister of public works.

"I'm impressed by the watch-dogs put in place to protect share-holders."

RETAIL STOCK ANALYST DON TIGERT,
AFTER ROBERT CAMPEAU WAS FORCED
TO RESTRUCTURE HIS DEBT-RIDDEN
ORGANIZATION IN SEPTEMBER 1989.
AT THE TIME, CAMPEAU STOCK WAS
SELLING FOR $19 PER SHARE.
BY JULY 1990, IT WAS SELLING FOR
$1.32 PER SHARE.

ASSESSING LABOUR'S PERFORMANCE

In their relationships with business and government, would you say unions are doing an excellent, good, only fair, or poor job in doing everything they can to...

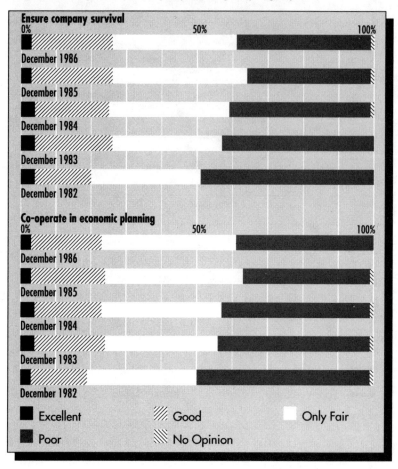

Ensure company survival

December 1986
December 1985
December 1984
December 1983
December 1982

Co-operate in economic planning

December 1986
December 1985
December 1984
December 1983
December 1982

■ Excellent   ▨ Good   ▢ Only Fair

■ Poor   ▧ No Opinion

1988 JAN.

Michel Côté, the federal minister of supply and services, is fired from the Conservative cabinet after failing to disclose a $250,000 personal loan from a friend and political backer who received government contracts.

1988 FEB.

RCMP officers charge five former executives of National Business Systems Inc. with perpetrating a $10-million fraud and theft.

1988 AUG.

Suzanne Blais-Grenier, a former junior minister in the Conservative government, is fired from the Tory caucus after charging that kickbacks are widespread in the distribution of government contracts.

MEASURES OF TRUST – LABOUR UNIONS
(Net Ratings)

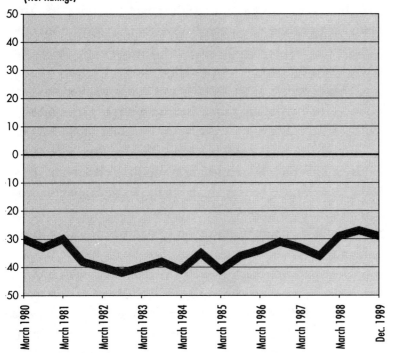

FACTS

In 1981, there were 11.4 million Roman Catholics in Canada, representing 47.3% of the population. There were 9.9 million Protestants, repre-senting 41.2%. Agnostics and atheists constituted the next largest group: 7.4%. Eastern Orthodox religions accounted for 1.5% of the popu-lation; Jews for 1.2%; and other religions for a total of 1.3%.

1988 DEC.

Michel Gravel, a Quebec Conservative MP, pleads guilty to 15 charges of seeking or accepting bribes in connection with the construc-tion of the National Museum of Civiliza-tion in Hull. Sen-tenced to two years in jail and given a $50,000 fine, Gravel serves two months.

1989 FEB.

Patricia Starr, presi-dent of a charitable organization, is accused of acting as conduit for more than $100,000 in illegal donations to Ontario politicians. The money comes from Tridel Enterprises, a large property devel-oper.In April 1990, Starr is charged with fraud.

1989 MARCH

Michael Milken, re-puted genius behind the rise of the junk-bond phenomenon that fuelled takeover fever on Wall Street in the 1980s, is charged with 98 counts of fraud by federal prosecutors. In April 1990, Milken pleaded guilty to six felony charges, and paid $600 million in fines.

> "They [the priests] need and have a right to the acceptance and understanding of the community in order to help them be restored to wholeness."
>
> JAMES HAYES, PRESIDENT OF THE CANADIAN CONFERENCE OF CATHOLIC BISHOPS, ON THE CONTROVERSY OVER PEDOPHILIA IN THE ROMAN CATHOLIC CHURCH, 1989

Newfoundland, where an inquiry into police handling of sexual-abuse charges at the Mount Cashel orphanage was under way.

The decade was less kind to the country's educators. True, Canadians think our educational system sets us apart from other nations; 78% said in March 1988 that it is one of the things that make Canada the best place to live. In addition, 58% said the education young people received today was either good or excellent. And most held favourable impressions of both primary- and high-school teachers. But a growing minority was far more skeptical.

Once, teachers were venerated, held up as community models, sought out for counselling beyond the classroom. In the 1980s, they came to be seen increasingly as trade unionists, concerned more about fringe benefits than about curriculum. Indeed, the general loss of faith in education since the Second World War is nothing short of remarkable. Many Canadians believe the education their parents received was better than their own; and they think their own was better than that their children are now receiving. Raised to believe that a good education was the key to success, they spent up to twenty years in school only to find that a Ph.D. in anthropology qualified one to become a government bureaucrat.

In fact, in only two areas – physical education and curriculum – did a clear majority rate the school system's performance as good or excellent. In seven other categories, from teaching the basics to preparing students for the workforce, most respondents assessed the system as only fair or poor. For many Canadians, the root of the problems in the schools is the failure to properly teach reading, writing, and arithmetic. And the answer, in their view, is to abandon the laissez-faire approach to education that gained popularity in the 1960s and return to a regimen of strict discipline that emphasized basic skills and core social values. In terms of net confidence ratings, our schools began the decade at +17 and ended it at +3.

Some institutions lost public confidence during the recession – then regained it as the economy recovered. This was true both for the media (newspapers and television) and for the courts. It was less true for organized religion, which earned a -9 rating in March 1990, compared to a +6 mark in March 1980. The lapse was most pronounced among men, those with only elementary education, residents of Ontario and the Atlantic provinces, and the middle-aged (45-54). Residents of the country said they were becoming more religious; residents of the city said they were becoming less so. And 46% of Quebeckers said religion was of less importance to them now than it had once been. Like the erosion of confidence in politics and business, labour unions, and education, the erosion of religious faith in the 1980s reflected a population that had lost its grip on the old verities and was searching in disparate ways for new ones.

In short, the problem Canadians confronted at the end of the decade was that, with too few exceptions, no institution could be relied on to provide what previous generations expected as a birthright: the simple assurance that traditional values still had meaning because they worked. The 1980s taught us repeatedly that they didn't work, that a new process was required to invest old values with new meaning – and that the current generation of leaders in virtually every field lacked the ability to create it.

INTO THE NINETIES

Despite all the evidence to the contrary, many Canadians want to believe that the old norms and the old rules still work. Made cynics by hard experience, we nonetheless cultivate private little gardens of hope. So while the erosion of public confidence in traditional institutions will continue in the decade ahead, politicians, businessmen, or religious leaders who manage to carve a new mould may be able to seize the public imagination.

In the political realm, we may see a candidate for office who maintains that he or she doesn't believe in conventional politics, will not speak to partisan audiences, and will declare all conflicts of interest. In the world of advertising, we may see commercials that do what they have seldom done – tell the truth about products. In the universe of corporate philanthropy, we may see chief executives who avoid preaching, for example, a "deep and abiding commitment to curing Alzheimer's disease." Canadians do not take such avowals seriously any more. Instead, they would believe the CEO who, acknowledging that ethics is good marketing, donated a percentage of gross sales to charity.

In the past, leadership was a calculated balance between empathy and deference. Canadians needed to respect and revere

FACTS

B.C. was Canada's most godless province: 20.5% of its residents said they belonged to no religion. Newfoundland was the most devout: only 1% said they had no religious preference.

MEASURES OF TRUST – SCHOOLS
(Net Ratings)

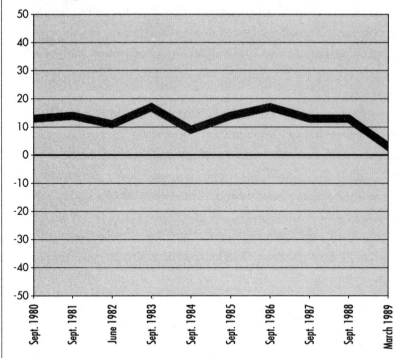

MEASURES OF TRUST – RELIGION
(Net Ratings)

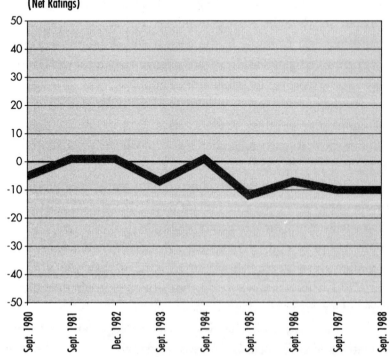

A REPORT CARD ON EDUCATION (MARCH 1988)

Does the education system do an excellent,
good, only fair, or poor job in...

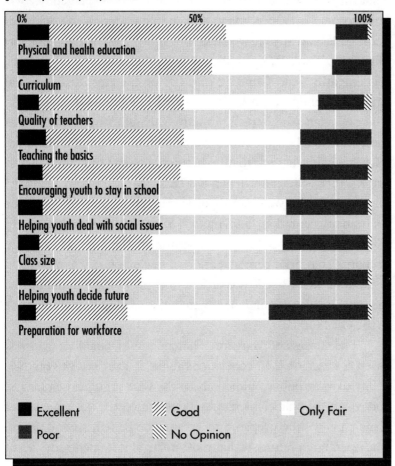

0%   50%   100%

Physical and health education

Curriculum

Quality of teachers

Teaching the basics

Encouraging youth to stay in school

Helping youth deal with social issues

Class size

Helping youth decide future

Preparation for workforce

■ Excellent   ▨ Good   □ Only Fair

■ Poor   ▧ No Opinion

FACTS

**Overall attendance at church and synagogue in Canada in 1965: 55%
In 1975: 41%
In 1985: 32%**

1989 APRIL

A five-member panel of inquiry is convened in Newfoundland by the Roman Catholic Church to probe allegations of sexual abuse of boys by priests and members of the Christian Brothers Order in a church-run orphanage.

1989 MAY

Quebec Conservative MP Richard Grisé pleads guilty to three counts of fraud and eight counts of breach of trust. Grisé is sentenced to one day in jail, three years' probation and a $20,000 fine (less than half his proceeds from bribes).

1989 JUNE

The Ontario Securities Commission drops charges against former B.C. Premier Bill Bennett, his brother Russell, and Herb Doman, chairman of Doman Industries, after a B.C. court acquits them of insider trading.

their politicians, their clergymen, and their captains of industry. But we also needed to have some sense of personal character – of what they'd be like to have to dinner. In the 1990s, deference will be obsolete. Canadians know too well that leaders aren't deities or demi-gods, and anyone who pretends otherwise will pay some sort of penalty. The only thing that will sell – apart from performance – is empathy. Jean Chrétien may not be the smooth talker that Brian Mulroney is, but he is all the more credible because of it. The politician who is ready to admit his fallibility – that he has sometimes laughed at ethnic jokes or even told them; that he's had a few speeding tickets; that he has occasionally had too much to drink – that politician will win our trust.

Indeed, the watchwords of leadership in the 1990s will be spontaneity, emotion, and motive. In 1972, Senator Edmund Muskie cried in public while running in the New Hampshire primary. That brief demonstration of raw emotion was a de facto declaration that Muskie was unfit for the presidency. In the 1990s, the same display of vulnerability might be enough to put someone in the Oval Office.

The success of Margaret Thatcher and Ronald Reagan was based as much on their convictions about policies as it was on their ability to sway public opinion about the wisdom of those policies. Today, unless politicians convey honest motives, no audience of Canadians will be prepared to extend the benefit of any doubt. The operating premise is that most political statements are lies of expediency, especially those delivered by men in blue suits who read from teleprompters on make-believe sets adorned with national flags. In the 1990s, it will be smart politics to confess mistakes, to admit ignorance, and to listen, not to speak.

The same test will apply in business. Private interest must not violate the public trust. It will not be enough for forest-product companies to say that their first job is to plant trees, not to harvest them. To win back public trust, they will have to be seen to be reforesting – and in numbers that will make a difference. They may have to go further, creating provincial parks on their own landholdings, teaching conservation, allocating more resources to fighting forest fires. Facing a less trustful, less deferential population, the corporation that positions itself as caring about both the public good and its own private interests will lead the pack.

MEASURES OF TRUST - HEALTH CARE PROFESSIONALS

What is your impression of doctors and nurses?

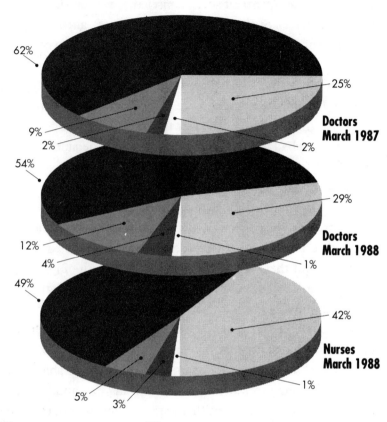

Doctors March 1987
- 62%
- 25%
- 9%
- 2%
- 2%

Doctors March 1988
- 54%
- 29%
- 12%
- 4%
- 1%

Nurses March 1988
- 49%
- 42%
- 5%
- 3%
- 1%

- ◼ Somewhat Favourable
- ◼ Somewhat Unfavourable
- ◻ No Opinion
- ◻ Very Favourable
- ◼ Very Unfavourable

1989 JULY

Donald Cormie and three other Principal Group officers are charged under the federal Competition Act. The charges were based on a provincial inquiry that found Cormie had acted fraudulently and dishonestly with investors in his trust companies.

1989 OCT.

American television evangelist Jim Bakker is convicted of defrauding members of the PTL Club of $3.7 million and sentenced to a 45-year jail term.

1989 NOV.

Conservative Senator Michel Cogger resigns from the Tory caucus after admitting that he wrote letters to a Crown corporation on his Montreal law firm's letterhead. The letters demanded payment for services, an apparent violation of Senate rules.

In the 1980s, the business community endorsed the principle of good works; in practice, it was much ignored. In the 1990s, companies that wear their social conscience on their sleeves will be the beneficiaries. Such a policy need not be mere altruism. In fact, corporate philanthropy can be sound marketing. When consumers are convinced that all competing mass-merchandised products are basically the same, the seller needs a new rationale for being chosen. It might be nothing more complicated than the provision of babysitting services, or the fact that the store manager coaches the local baseball team. The institution that understands why the erosion of trust in traditional authority is occurring will be best prepared to win it back – not by preaching old formulae, but by putting something genuinely new in the window.

Similarly, the religious leader who can help people find Christian-Judaic answers to their problems may be able to refill the churches. But there will be no credibility in continuing to preach the traditional totems and superstitions – the wrath of an all-powerful and vengeful God. In fact, what might succeed in the 1990s is a church of the vernacular, the gospel of which might be nothing more than good sportsmanship and other rules to live by.

The challenge for labour unions will be to establish a role beyond the framework of the 9 to 5 working day and to address quality of life considerations that are increasingly important to its members. Like every other major institution in Canadian life, unions must finally accept that the world has changed – that children no longer work in coal mines, that the minimum wage is not a pressing concern, and that, as New Democratic party leader Audrey McLaughlin once said, capital is too important to leave to capitalists. To regain relevance, labour leaders must abandon knee-jerk adversarial politics, partisan commitments, and their exclusive focus on the workplace. Only those unions that offer new approaches to old problems and are willing to play a broader, less partisan role will be able to renew the faith of the rank and file.

In the classrooms, the solutions are less clear cut. The system now is torn between strict traditionalists, who want to revert to teaching fundamentals, and laissez-faire innovators, who want to take the next step forward. Canadians generally prefer the more familiar terrain of the three Rs. Convinced that the present curriculum provides an inferior education to the one our parents had, we are deeply skeptical about more innovation. We don't know what the next step is and we doubt that it will work.

On the other hand, many Canadians believe that the root causes of society's problems have less to do with the grammar of English or French than with the grammar of morality. And what we really want the schools to do – particularly at the elementary level – is teach values, not skills. Thus, if and when the conflict between education as discipline and education as experience plays itself out, schools could become quasi-religious training grounds that teach the pragmatism of ethics. The good Samaritan can still be a contemporary role model, not because he is his brother's keeper, but because in the modern world he, too, is likely to need a helping hand one day.

The universities have a quite different problem: to end their self-imposed isolation from Canadian society. They must begin doing research that has practical application in the communities from which they draw financial support. Some institutions have already done so; most have not. The universities must also recognize that education is not simply an adolescent experience, but a lifetime exercise – particularly in a society which understands that change is constant and in which nearly seven out of ten Canadians say they would benefit from training in their present jobs.

The larger question, for all traditional institutions, is what style of leadership will emerge in the decade ahead. Given current attitudes, it is probable that many leaders will reject traditional career paths, choosing to run the YMCA rather than any political organization; or to head a small out-of-the-home consulting firm instead of a major corporation. What Canadians wanted in the 1980s were changes in process, not result. They wanted a system – in politics, in business, in education – demonstrably more responsive to changing needs. And they wanted leaders who understood that a new language was required, and knew how to speak it. The current generation of leaders was unable to deliver. It seems inevitable that the next generation, socialized in the 1970s, will have a different, more contemporary mind-set, and will be more in tune with public opinion and attitudes. Too much is at stake for that not to occur.

URBAN BLUES

CHAPTER 4

"Towered cities please us then, And the busy hum of men."
JOHN MILTON, "L'ALLEGRO," 1631

"There's a mood in the city that events are not in people's control, that their ability to influence what's going on is small."
JOHN SEWELL, FORMER MAYOR OF TORONTO

"The States serves as an early-warning system for Canada. We can look down and see what's happening in New York and Cleveland and then try to avoid the same thing happening here. But it's not easy, because the same destructive forces are at work in Canada."
JANE JACOBS, 1972

CANADIAN MYTHOLOGY GLORIFIES OUR NATURAL HERITAGE –THE uncorrupted, largely uninhabited great outdoors. In reality, of course, the majority of Canadians have little or no contact with that vast, rugged wilderness of forests and lakes. We are, overwhelmingly, an urban society. Some 80% of the population live in just twelve cities. About 30% live in the three largest urban centres – Toronto, Montreal, and Vancouver. Yet, as the 1980s drew to a close, there was gathering evidence that more and more people were no longer pleased by the "busy hum of men" in the "towered cities."

Indeed, the city was increasingly associated with trends utterly abhorrent to many city-dwellers. Among them: the absurd cost of living, most palpably expressed in exorbitant house prices and inflated rents; rising levels of crime, both petty and violent;

BODILY HARM   The 1980s saw an explosion in violent, often drug-related crime in the major urban centres, prompting many worried Canadians to question whether they were safe even in their own neighbourhoods.

"I've made a quality-of-life decision."

DOCTOR RAY TERVO, AFTER LEAVING TORONTO FOR SASKATCHEWAN IN 1989

"It's going to be traffic hell."

PIERRE BERTON, ON THE FUTURE OF TORONTO, 1989

environmental stresses, which ran the gamut from garbage disposal to smog to traffic congestion; and visible demographic change, the result of the arrival of Canada's first genuine wave of non-white immigration.

The early morning newscasts on any given day in the 1980s would probably have touched on all these problems and more: traffic watchers in helicopters advising commuters that rush-hour gridlock had begun; weather forecasters measuring the projected pollution index; police reporters chronicling overnight break-ins, hold-ups, drug busts, murders (and only skimming the surface of the real numbers); city hall commentators bemoaning the shortage of rental housing; and social-affairs correspondents issuing renewed pleas for donations to the city's food bank for the homeless.

Canadians reacted to these developments in predictable ways. Many abandoned the large metropolises – or contemplated doing so – for smaller centres, where housing was cheaper and commuting was a term reserved for prison sentences. (In fact, when asked in 1986 and again in 1988 whether, given a choice, they would elect to live in the country instead of the city, almost 70% of the sample chose the country.) And those who stayed in larger cities – the majority – began to seriously question the quality of their lives and their legacy to their children.

This soul-searching produced a variety of responses, if not answers. In an environment that seemed increasingly threatened by gratuitous crime, Canadians sought to protect themselves. They installed security alarms in their homes. They studied martial arts and learned self-defence. They bought guns. They avoided certain quadrants of the city after dark. And they organized their neighbours to be crime-spotters and to protect their children.

In fact, the lives of most Canadians – even those living in the heart of the cities and buying the newest, high-tech burglar alarms – were basically untouched by the trends they feared most: random, violent crime, escalating drug use, crushing poverty. But the abstractness of the threat did not diminish it. In a poll taken in the spring of 1984, some 44% of respondents agreed with the statement – "I don't feel safe when I go out alone at night in my neighbourhood." Naturally, the larger the community in which the respondent lived, the likelier the agreement. And – again not surprisingly – women and senior citizens were far likelier than men

WHERE DO YOU LIVE?

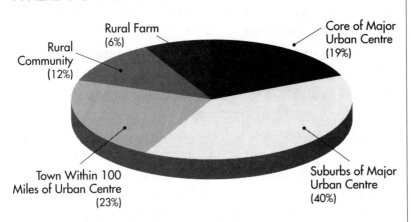

Rural Farm
(6%)

Rural
Community
(12%)

Core of Major
Urban Centre
(19%)

Town Within 100
Miles of Urban Centre
(23%)

Suburbs of Major
Urban Centre
(40%)

WHERE WOULD YOU PREFER TO LIVE?

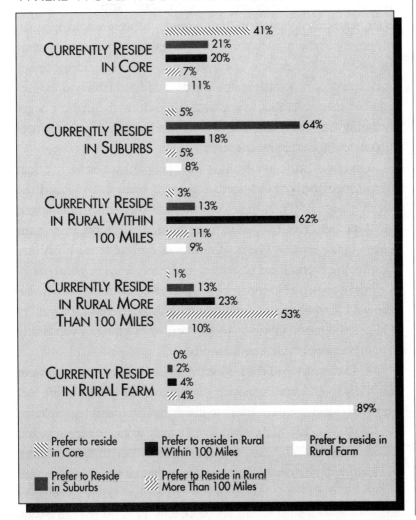

CURRENTLY RESIDE
IN CORE
- 41%
- 21%
- 20%
- 7%
- 11%

CURRENTLY RESIDE
IN SUBURBS
- 5%
- 64%
- 18%
- 5%
- 8%

CURRENTLY RESIDE
IN RURAL WITHIN
100 MILES
- 3%
- 13%
- 62%
- 11%
- 9%

CURRENTLY RESIDE
IN RURAL MORE
THAN 100 MILES
- 1%
- 13%
- 23%
- 53%
- 10%

CURRENTLY RESIDE
IN RURAL FARM
- 0%
- 2%
- 4%
- 4%
- 89%

Prefer to reside
in Core

Prefer to reside in Rural
Within 100 Miles

Prefer to reside in
Rural Farm

Prefer to Reside
in Suburbs

Prefer to Reside in Rural
More Than 100 Miles

FACTS

**Percentage of
Canada's population
that lived in the 12
largest cities in 1981:
almost 76
Percentage in
1986: 80
Percentage of adult
city dwellers living in
inner cities: 62
Percentage living in
suburbia: 38**

**Decline in population
of the Island of
Montreal in the past
15 years: 200,000
Rise in population of
off-island suburbs
and cities in same
period: 350,000**

to fear a casual stroll in their neighbourhoods after dark, women and senior citizens being principal victims of exactly that sort of random, predatory crime.

But holding to the thesis that the moral quality of urban life had decayed, most Canadians believed nevertheless that their own cities and neighbourhoods had not essentially changed in the past few years – if anything, they thought they had improved.

In September 1989, Decima asked Canadians to assess twenty-three separate aspects of community life – from the quality of police forces to the availability and cost of health care; from the friendliness of people to the cost of owning or renting a home; from the quality of education to the number of poor and homeless. Respondents were specifically asked whether, in the last two or three years, these categories had gotten significantly or somewhat better, significantly or somewhat worse – or were unchanged. In only seven of the twenty-three categories did a majority or near-majority think things were worse: violent crime; use of illegal drugs; youth behaviour; pollution; and the cost and availability of houses and apartments. In fact, home ownership drew the highest negative rating; 71% said the cost of owning a home had made ownership more difficult in recent years.

On most other issues, however, people saw either distinct improvement or no fundamental change. Indeed, 87% said the overall quality of life in their communities was either unchanged (44%) or better (43%). What constituted the most important quality-of-life issues? The community as a place to raise families or retire, the friendliness of people, and safety from physical harm. In other words, the trends people perceived as most worrisome were not the trends that dominated their evaluations of the quality of life. If the moral fabric of society was unravelling, it was doing so in other people's neighbourhoods.

It was residents of the largest urban cities, of course, who were least likely to endorse the notion that the overall quality of life had improved – and the most likely to insist that problems like violence and illegal-drug use had grown significantly worse in recent years. For example, 36% of those living in cities of one million or more said that their personal safety was somewhat or significantly more at risk now than it was two or three years earlier. Of those living in cities of between 50,000 and 100,000, only 17% felt the same way.

COST OF LIVING

Cost of a cheap two-bedroom apartment in Montreal in 1988: $455 a month

In Toronto: $770 a month

Cost of a luxury two-bedroom apartment in Montreal in 1988: $710 a month

In Toronto: $1,525 a month

Value of resale homes in Toronto in 1980: $75,620

In 1989: $273,698

Value of resales in suburban Mississauga, Ont., in 1980: $80,340

In 1989: $135,221

Decline in value of resales in Edmonton between 1980 and 1988: $2,500

Percentage of one person's pre-tax income needed to carry mortgage, property taxes, and utilities on an average detached bungalow in Toronto in 1989: 75

Percentage needed to carry it in 1985: 41

Percentage needed to carry a comparable home in Vancouver in 1989: 65

In 1985: 51

(The figures are based on a 25% down payment and a 25-year mortgage at a fixed five-year term)

1981 JAN.

The first food bank in Canada opens in Edmonton. Over the next four years, dozens more open across the country.

1981 OCT.

RCMP seize a shipment of methaqualone worth an estimated $200 million at an airport in Collingwood, Ont. It is to that point the largest drug seizure in Canadian history.

1983 JAN.

New Criminal Code amendments create three new categories of sexual assault. For the first time, husbands and wives may lay charges against each other.

FACTS

The cost of a kilogram of cocaine in Peru in 1989: $250

The wholesale cost of the kilo in Toronto: $35,000-$45,000

The retail cost of the kilo: $350,000-$400,000

Value of sales of illicit drugs in Canada in 1988, according to RCMP: more than $10 billion

Number of drug addicts the city of Vancouver expected to turn in used needles when it began issuing new ones in an anti-AIDS campaign in early 1989: 200

Number who have turned in used needles since then: 3,000

"I thought one shot would do it, so I was surprised when he got up and walked toward me. He was big, he weighed three hundred pounds, so I shot him again and he yelled and opened his jacket and fell forward. I didn't forget the last shot to the head."

RENÉ SIMARD, ON WHAT IT WAS LIKE TO KILL HIS FIRST VICTIM, A MAFIOSO NAMED MICHEL MARION

RATING YOUR COMMUNITY (SEPTEMBER 1989)

How has your community changed in the past 2 or 3 years?

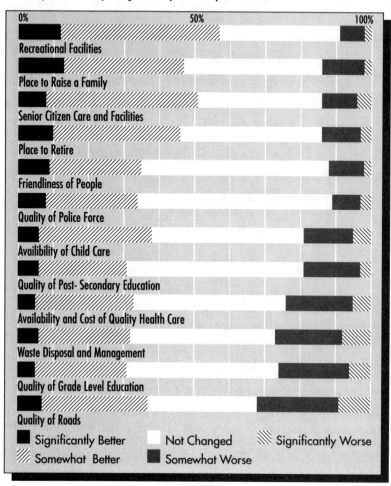

Recreational Facilities

Place to Raise a Family

Senior Citizen Care and Facilities

Place to Retire

Friendliness of People

Quality of Police Force

Availibility of Child Care

Quality of Post-Secondary Education

Availability and Cost of Quality Health Care

Waste Disposal and Management

Quality of Grade Level Education

Quality of Roads

■ Significantly Better   □ Not Changed   ▨ Significantly Worse
▨ Somewhat Better   ■ Somewhat Worse

1986 SEPT.
Prime Minister Brian Mulroney calls the heroin problem in Canada a drug epidemic.

1987 FEB.
The Canadian Sentencing Commission says Canadians have lost confidence in the criminal-justice system.

1987 MAY
Ottawa unveils a $210-million five-year national drug strategy; 70% is allocated for education and rehabilitation.

RATING YOUR COMMUNITY (SEPTEMBER 1989)

How has your community changed in the past 2 or 3 years?

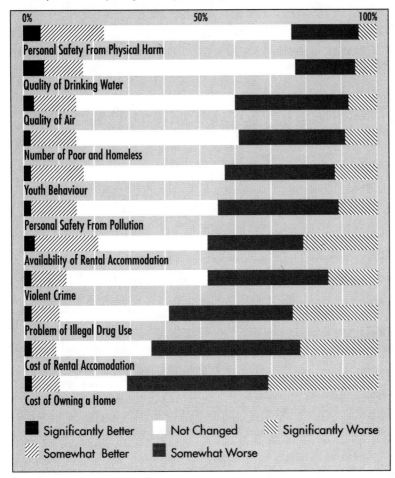

Personal Safety From Physical Harm
Quality of Drinking Water
Quality of Air
Number of Poor and Homeless
Youth Behaviour
Personal Safety From Pollution
Availability of Rental Accommodation
Violent Crime
Problem of Illegal Drug Use
Cost of Rental Accomodation
Cost of Owning a Home

- ■ Significantly Better
- □ Not Changed
- ▨ Significantly Worse
- ▧ Somewhat Better
- ■ Somewhat Worse

FACTS

**Percentage of murders committed in Canada that are the result of a dispute: 80
Percentage that are for money: 10
Percentage that are for sex: 5
Percentage committed by the emotionally disturbed: 5**

**Percentage of all crime committed in Canada that is non-violent: 92
Of the remaining 8%, most are simple assault in which no weapons are involved and no bodily harm is inflicted.**

Although the incidence of violent crime is rising, up 17% between 1982 and 1986, more serious offences – homicide, attempted murder, aggravated sexual assault, and robbery – have actually declined in number.

1987 JUNE

Steven Kesler, a Calgary druggist, is acquitted on charges of second-degree murder, after a 12-day trial. Kesler shot and killed a man attempting to rob his drugstore.

1989 JAN.

New federal legislation makes money laundering an indictable offence and permits the seizure of assets of convicted criminals.

1989 MARCH

Toronto police report an outbreak of swarming incidents, in which gangs of marauding youths (in groups as large as 150) surround a victim in malls or in subways demanding money, jewellery or clothes. Those who refuse are beaten up. Police order a crackdown.

"A society with too many killings is one that ultimately flirts with civil war."

NEIL WOOD, IN *THE LAST DANCE, MURDER IN CANADA*

"People tend to think a lot of violent crime is committed by criminals out on parole. This is another myth. If you abolished parole, it would not have a significant impact on the violent-crime rate."

SOLICITOR GENERAL JAMES KELLEHER IN 1987

FOOD BANKS

Number of food banks in existence in Canada in 1980: 0
Number in existence in 1989: 130

Number of children in Metro Toronto who used food banks in 1989: 1 in 7
Number of welfare recipients using Toronto food banks for emergency grocery assistance in 1989: 43,660 a month
Total number of those seeking assistance from Toronto food banks in February 1990: 81,000

Number of those needing food banks in Toronto in 1986: 42,000
Number needing them in 1989: 84,000

What food-bank recipients on welfare in Toronto had left for food, clothing, shelter, and medicine after paying for housing in 1989: $22 a week

Estimated number of Canadians receiving food and hot meals from food banks and soup kitchens every month in 1989: 378,000
Percentage that were children: 40

Estimated number of homeless Canadians in 1989: 250,000
Estimated number on waiting list for subsidized public housing in Toronto in 1989: 10,000

RISE OF THE UNDERCLASS   In 1980 food banks for the hungry were virtually non-existent in Canada. By the end of the decade, however, they were numerous and permanent fixtures in most of our cities.

GRIDLOCKS

Eight out of ten Canadian households now own cars, trucks, or vans. And almost 40% own more than one vehicle.

Estimated cost annually of traffic congestion in Toronto in lost time, productivity, etc.: $1.9 billion

Average number of people carried in a car in Toronto rush hours in 1989: 1.3

Number of passengers carried by the Toronto Transit Commission in 1980: 366.4 million
Number carried in 1989: 450.7 million

Number of stop-lights in Calgary in 1980: 388
Number in 1989: 525

Maximum number of cars Montreal's Metropolitan Boulevard expressway was designed to carry per day when it was built in the late 1950s: 100,000
Number it carried in 1989: 145,000

Number of traffic accidents in Vancouver reported to police in 1980: 28,616
Number reported in 1989: 34,393

Number of automobiles registered in Canada in 1970: 6.6 million
Number registered in 1988: 12 million
Number of drivers licensed in Canada in 1980: 13.8 million
Number licensed in 1988: 17 million

FACTS

**Number of violent crimes per 100,000 population in Ottawa in 1980: 665
Number in 1987: 958
Number of violent crimes per 100,000 population in Toronto in 1980: 666
Number in 1987: 1,121**

**Percentage of all violent-crime charges laid against men in 1986: 76
Percentage laid against women: 8
Percentage laid against young offenders: 16**

Generally, the larger the city, the more violent crime. On the other hand, levels of violent crime are rising 10% faster in smaller centres (towns of less than 10,000) than they are in cities of more than 250,000.

"The problem is very simple. The prisons can't handle the numbers."

DAVID COLE, A TORONTO LAWYER WHO SPECIALIZES IN PRISON LAW

"You can't solve the youth problem with the Young Offenders Act and handcuffs. You really have to get at the social root of the problem."

CARYL ARUNDEL, POLICY DIRECTOR, METRO TORONTO COMMUNITY SERVICES DEPARTMENT, APRIL 1989

WHAT'S GETTING WORSE?

Assessments by residents of cities of more than 1 million

% Somewhat/Significantly Worse

	More Than One Million	Vancouver	Toronto	Montreal
Cost of a home	84	93	87	71
Cost of rental accommodation	79	84	86	63
Use of illegal drugs	65	63	72	89
Availability of rental accommodation	63	77	79	24
Violent crime	63	67	71	58
Safety from pollution	58	61	66	46
Air quality	56	57	62	49
Numer of poor/homeless	55	61	56	47
Behaviour of young people	49	43	60	43

1989 APRIL

Charles Yacoub, a Lebanese immigrant, hijacks a New York-bound bus in Montreal, forces it to drive to Ottawa and holds 11 passengers and the driver hostage on Parliament Hill for eight hours before surrendering. In April 1990, Yacoub receives a six-year prison sentence.

1989 MAY

The RCMP say Canada is a shipping centre for South American drugs. The same month, Montreal police seize 500 kilograms of cocaine — in individually wrapped 1-kg packets — that was flown non-stop in a twin-engine plane from Colombia. Street value of the cocaine: $25 million.

1989 JUNE

Concluding a criminal case that lasted for years, Robert Rowbotham is sentenced to serve 17 years for importing and trafficking in marijuana and hashish.

What's Getting Better?

Assessments by residents of cities of more than 1 million

% Somewhat/Significantly Better

	More Than One Million	Vancouver	Toronto	Montreal
Recreational facilities	59	57	61	54
Quality of roads	41	43	41	31
Senior citizen's facilities	40	35	37	51
Place to raise a family	39	41	37	41
Quality of police force	37	33	43	29
Place to retire	37	39	29	48
Availability of child care	35	32	36	34
Quality of waste management	34	27	33	37
Friendliness of people	31	27	27	37
Quality of health care	31	27	32	36
Quality of post-secondary education	27	30	28	21
Quality of grade level education	26	23	31	20

1989 SEPT.
New Brunswick police and RCMP seize a cache of weapons and more than 3,000 rounds of ammunition in arresting four South Americans in Edmundston. There is speculation that the group was intent on freeing two jailed pilots who had attempted to smuggle $250 million worth of cocaine into the country earlier in the year.

1989 DEC.
Fourteen women engineering students at the University of Montreal are shot to death by Marc Lepine.

1989 DEC.
The Halifax food bank gives notice that it will close on Jan. 1, 1994, attempting to force civic officials to address the continuing problem of hunger.

FACTS

The overall level of drug crime in Canada was lower in 1987 than it was in 1980. In 1980, there were about 309 drug crimes committed per 100,000 population. In the next six years, the number dropped to 220 (per 100,000 population), then rose again in 1987 to 241.

Number of drug offences recorded by police in Canada in 1987: 62,000
Percentage this represented of all recorded crime: 2
Percentage of drug cases that involved cannabis: 70

Number of drug crimes involving cocaine in 1980: 1,700
Number in 1987: 8,200

"I'm not saying I'm really into Hitler, but you've got to admire the guy. He liked filling his campaigns with a lot of people. You get enough people together, you're not just a person in the crowd. You are the crowd. You're invincible! Gangs are very close to Hitler that way. He was a brilliant philosopher."

A YOUNG TORONTO GANG MEMBER, AUGUST 1989

Similarly, respondents who lived in cities of a million plus were twice as likely to think their community was not an attractive place to raise a family as those who lived in cities of less than 50,000.

In fact, although almost 60% of the nation lives either in the core of major urban centres or in their suburbs, a clear majority (57%) would rather live elsewhere – either within a hundred miles of the cities or in more rural communities. Only 41% of those who reside in the very core of the largest cities actually want to live there; 21% would opt for the suburbs and 20% would choose to commute, living within a hundred miles. In sharp contrast, 89% of respondents living on farms want to stay right where they are.

This phenomenon cannot be seen in isolation. Increasingly concerned about quality of life, increasingly less beguiled by the sirens of ambition or acquisition, more and more citizens of the megalopolis – particularly yuppies and baby-boomers – are looking elsewhere for answers. Drugs, violence, poverty, house prices, the homeless, even pollution may not scar them directly, but the aggregate weight of these mounting problems consti-tutes a psychological burden of which urban Canadians would like to be relieved. This analysis applies especially to married people, a majority of whom would prefer not to live in core urban areas. In fact, the more children in the family, the greater the desire to live in smaller communities.

A notable counter-trend exists among senior citizens, who voice a greater preference for returning to large urban centres – probably reflecting the availability of superior health care and other facilities for the aged, particularly transportation. And yet, in the 1980s, the centres of our largest cities were filling up with young, well-educated, professional, single men and women.

At the end of the decade, the cores of Canada's major cities were increasingly populated by the oldest and the youngest, the richest and the poorest, the upwardly – and the downwardly – mobile. The extremes were not as stark as in New York or Wash-ington or Chicago, but the basic demographic drift was inescap-able. Canadian cities, more and more, belonged to those who lived on the financial and moral margins of society – and to that minor-ity affluent enough to insulate itself from what was happening all around it. The middle class was there, but its numbers were shrinking dramatically – gone to the suburbs, where housing was

WHAT IS IT?

SMERFS: The name given to drug couriers employed to turn over drug money in a series of bank transactions before it arrives, cleansed of its origins, in an off-shore tax haven.

CRACK: A combination of cocaine and baking soda, crack is smoked. A pill-sized dose sells for $10-40. It provides an instant high that quickly fades.

ICE: Ice (sometimes known as speed) is crystallized methamphetamine. Users smoke it. The vapour is absorbed by the brain, producing a high that reportedly lasts for several hours. Odourless and colourless, ice is said to be more addictive than cocaine. Cost of a gram: between $250 and $400 (US) in 1989.

T&R: Talwin and Ritalin. These are prescription drugs that are illegally manufactured and injected. They are sometimes called the poor man's heroin.

TO GROW OR NOT TO GROW
Measuring attitudes toward urban development

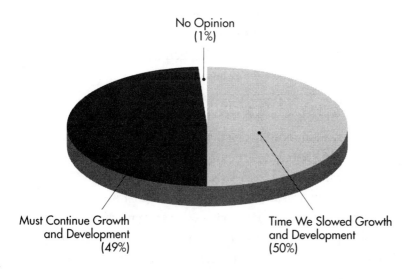

No Opinion
(1%)

Must Continue Growth
and Development
(49%)

Time We Slowed Growth
and Development
(50%)

FACTS

Estimated percentage of drug offences involving simple possession in 1987: 67
Percentage involving trafficking: 30

Number of admissions for treatment of drug problems in Alberta in 1989: 37,000
Percentage of adult Albertans reporting in 1989 that they or someone in their family have had substance-abuse problems: 30

Victoria, B.C., once known as the retirement capital of Canada, is also the drug-offence leader among major Canadian cities. In 1987, it recorded 676 offences per 100,000 population. Vancouver wasn't far behind, at 598. Those figures compare with 301 for Toronto and about 125 for Montreal.

more affordable, the threat of wanton crime and rampaging, drug-induced youth gangs more distant, the plight of the homeless more remote, the traffic less sclerotic.

To some extent, the flight to suburbia was occasioned by economic necessity; when two-bedroom detached bungalows in midtown Vancouver were selling for $350,000, as they were in 1988, even a two-income, childless couple could no longer afford the carrying costs. But to some extent, the exodus had nothing to do with money and everything to do with how an increasing number of people wanted to live. They wanted to raise their families in clean, safe neighbourhoods, where people were friendly and the threat of harm in any form was negligible. Measured against that standard, the cities of Canada were increasingly found wanting.

INTO THE NINETIES

As the decade drew to a close, Canadians were becoming more serious and more introspective. Although we perceived ourselves as being different from Americans – and superior to them – our lives were increasingly the same. The contradiction was troubling and nowhere more apparent than in the cities. On the one hand, we believed we were more tolerant than Americans – that Canada was what President George Bush had in mind when he said he wanted to make the United States a kinder, gentler nation. On the other, the reported incidence of rape and violent assault, racism and illegal drug use had reached levels once associated with the inner ghettos of American cities.

If the facts refuted the thesis, something clearly had gone awry. It wasn't the infrastructure of Canadian cities – roads and bridges, schools and hospitals. If anything, most Canadians believed (often mistakenly) that the urban infrastructure was better than ever. What had gone awry was something less tangible and more pernicious – the behaviour of young people, the fear of violence, the deteriorating moral fibre of society itself, as well as the astronomical cost of home ownership.

Governments can cope with infrastructure problems. They can build new stadiums, expressways, schools and old-age homes. In the 1960s, we called that urban renewal. But the problems that will plague our cities in the 1990s can't be attacked in the same way. We already have legislation designed to prevent young people from smoking crack, swarming old women in parks, and throwing helpless immigrants in front of subway trains. But the traditional legislative solutions are inadequate. Governments can't grapple with moral and social decay. There is no federal ministry of state for urban affairs any more. Few in government even focus on urban issues, and those who do are concerned about infrastructure: harbour lands in Toronto or Expo lands in Vancouver. Hiring more police may help, but the added visibility of the police only underlines the problem.

Unless we find new ways to deal with these problems, we will see the increasing Manhattanization of our cities. The trend is already apparent. More and more, our inner cities are populated by those who can't afford to leave, the very rich and those who work for the rich. The middle class is being driven out. People may continue to feel comfortable in their communities for a while. They don't yet perceive the moral decay as occurring in their own neighbourhood; it's in East Vancouver or in East Montreal or at Jane and Finch in Toronto. But without concerted action – by governments, business, social agencies – it will encroach on more back yards. People will demand solutions that don't exist, and eventually they will be forced to leave.

In the quest for solutions, the best models are partnerships of public and private resources. Governments can't act alone: they have neither the know-how nor the money. Morality is increasingly perceived as a prerequisite of good business. Business people aren't just talking about good ethics; they're practising them. Of course, business has a more direct interest in the matter: if people abandon the cities, so does the workforce on which employers depend. What governments can do is set priorities and provide seed money. Business can lend expertise and hardware. Community groups can co-ordinate, deliver, and execute.

This model has enabled Frontier College to conduct a long, effective war on illiteracy. More recently, it has enabled the YMCA to create successful storefront businesses by providing the resources – lawyers and accountants donating time, computer firms donating hardware and software – that many small businesses lack. In fact, the YMCA storefronts are incubation centres,

FACTS

Crimes per 100,000 in 1988 rose along an East-West axis: Newfoundland: 5,180
Quebec: 7,228
Ontario: 8,835
The Prairies: 11,000
British Columbia: 13,604

In 1988, there were 565 homicides reported in Canada. That was the lowest number in more than a decade. Although most of these murders occurred in Ontario and Quebec, Alberta actually recorded the highest homicide rate – 3 per 100,000 population.

Percentage increase in crime on the Toronto Transit Commission between 1987 and 1988: 38
Percentage increase between 1988 and 1989: 13
Percentage increase in thefts between 1988 and 1989: 69
Percentage increase in assaults between 1988 and 1989: 19

"It's not unusual now to have cases involving firearms every day of the week. Something as simple as pulling over a stolen vehicle and finding every one of the occupants armed. That was totally foreign to us not so long ago."

STAFF SERGEANT MICHAEL SALE,
METRO TORONTO POLICE, 1990

NOT IN MY BACKYARD   An astonishing increase in municipal waste throughout the 1980s raised concern about the consumption habits of Canadians – and, more urgently, about where to dispose of their garbage.

creating jobs at a third of the cost of public works and about a fifti-eth of the cost of direct transfers. Philanthropist Martin Connell has another approach. In Canadian native communities, he offers loans to the one business regarded by the natives themselves as worthiest. Subsequent loans to other businesses are contingent upon the first recipient making six consecutive months of repay-ment. The community can't let him fail. By 1989, Connell had made more than a thousand such loans without a single default.

But private-public partnerships are not a panacea. Some problems will persist. Our young people may be the first generation in fifty years without its own role models; even its rock stars are forty years old. Feeling rejected by society, teenagers consider anti-social behaviour a statement of identity. Immigration, too, will change our cities in dramatic ways. By the end of the decade, Canada will be not only a multicultural society but a multiracial one as well. We must also come to grips with the question of home ownership, once considered a natural birthright of all Canadians. In the 1980s, as the cost of a single-family home soared out of reach, younger Canadians engaged in status substitution. Unable to save enough money to buy a home, they bought BMWs and Armani suits instead. It wasn't that they abandoned their goals; they simply found other ways to realize them.

The price of housing will continue to push many Canadians into the more affordable suburbs and satellite communities of major cities. But other economic factors are encouraging the urban exodus. One is what the futurist Alvin Toffler called the electronic cottage. With a computer, a fax machine, and a modem in the home, people no longer need to spend two unproductive, often stressful hours commuting to and from work. The second is the changing nature of the Canadian economy: increasingly, Canada produces services, not goods. A manufacturing sector – plants and factories – needs to be close to raw materials and to workers. A service sector doesn't.

Crime and drugs, fetid air and dubious drinking water, immigration and housing, too many cars and too many people, technology and economics: the themes that dominate private and public debate in Canada all find their centre, ultimately, in our cities. Which is why urban issues will be at the top of the national agenda in the 1990s.

FACTS

Number of hand-guns registered in Toronto in 1987: 63,071
Number, unregis-tered, estimated to be in private hands: 360,000

Number of calls involving guns answered by Toronto police in 1983: 84
Number in 1988: 235

There were approx-imately 26,600 inmates in federal and provincial penitentiaries in Canada in 1987. Percentage who were in jail for the first time: 62
Percentage likely to return: 30

The estimated amount of money earned by organized crime in Canada in 1984: $20 billion
Amount believed gen-erated by drugs: $9 billion

TURNING GREEN

CHAPTER 5

Hurt not the earth, neither the sea, nor the trees.

REVELATION VII:3

The first law of ecology is that everything is related to everything else.

BARRY COMMONER

THE OZONE LAYER AND THE GREENHOUSE EFFECT. BHOPAL AND Chernobyl. Acid rain and toxic waste. Putrid air, poisoned water. It was in the 1980s that Canadians in large numbers first recognized the fragility of nature. Recognition did not come quickly. As the decade began, other issues – the economy, rising crime rates, the nuclear-arms race, declining energy reserves, tensions in national unity – were considered more important. The environment? As a source of public anxiety, it was practically invisible.

Indeed, for the better part of the 1980s, Canadians were generally sanguine about the environment. In June 1986, a strong majority (62%) described the quality of the environment in their own area as either excellent (14%) or good (48%). Only 38% said it was fair or poor. But just three years later, when Decima asked the same question, the "excellent or good" quotient had fallen to 53%; the "fair or poor" total had climbed to 47% – a remarkable shift.

The same trend was apparent when people were asked directly whether the quality of the environment had improved or declined. In June 1985, 30% said it was either significantly or somewhat better; 24% said it was significantly or somewhat

OIL ON WATER   The Exxon Valdez disaster in April 1989 left 10 million
gallons of crude oil floating on Alaska's Prince William Sound –
an ecological catastrophe that heightened environmental concern.

"We have what I call a Quebec valve. We simply flush everything into the rivers and lakes."

MONTREAL ENGINEER PIERRE DESJARDINS, AUGUST 1981

worse. Four years later, only 24% said the environment in their area had improved; fully 36% said it had deteriorated.

As the years passed, the trend line continued to turn up – sharply. By the end of the decade, ecology had become the central preoccupation of Canadians. In fact, by September 1989, economic issues aside, more of us identified the environment as the single most important problem facing the nation than the combined total of those citing international affairs, national unity, and social/moral issues.

Beyond mere environmental aesthetics or the protection of endangered species, what helped push the green agenda to centre stage was the perception – stronger as the years passed – that pollution was not only injurious to the natural world at large; it was also damaging our health. If the St. Lawrence beluga whale and the bald eagle were endangered species, then so was humanity itself. In June 1982, Decima asked Canadians how much pollution affected the health of their families; 53% said very much or a fair amount. Seven years later, in response to a similar question, the figure was 81%. Indeed, on one specific issue – the increase in non-biodegradable waste – some 25% said it posed an "immediate life-threatening risk." Not true, of course – but a telling indication nevertheless.

Not surprisingly, those of us who lived in large, heavily industrialized urban areas were more likely than others to link environmental problems to human health. But our expressions of concern were not mere abstractions. In the summer of 1989, seven people out of ten said that environmental considerations had actually made them change their behaviour – what they bought, what they consumed. An even greater number – 76% – conceded that personal sacrifices would be needed to protect the environment.

We recognized that such sacrifices would inevitably have economic costs. But even in the depths of the recession in the early 1980s, respondents said that safeguarding the environment was more important than, say, saving jobs or economic growth. We acknowledged, for example, that stricter environmental laws might force affected industries to raise prices. But even in June 1982, with the nation gripped by recession, 79% attached the higher priority to the environment.

OUR MOST IMPORTANT PROBLEMS
What issue concerns you the most?

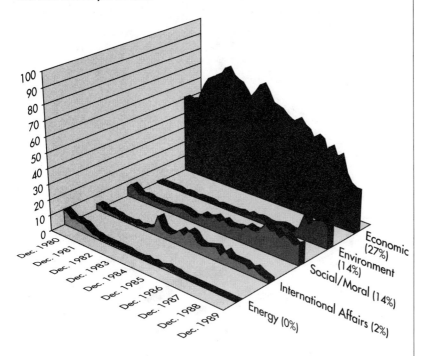

FACTS

More than 30% of Canada's urban sewage is untreated. In Quebec, for example, only 250 of 1,500 municipalities have sewage-treatment facilities. Half of the sewage in Montreal – a city of over 2 million – goes directly into the St. Lawrence River.

Level of lead in children's blood considered serious by Toronto public-health officials: 20 micrograms per decilitre Level of lead found in 21-month-old Daniel Claus-Nesbitt's blood in June 1987: 68 mpd (his family lived near a Toronto lead smelter)

1980 JUNE	**1980** JULY	**1981** SEPT.
After years of protest by environmentalists, Canada announces that it will withdraw from membership in the International Whaling Commission. Canada ceased commercial whaling operations in 1972.	Ottawa extends an earlier ban on PCBs to cover all new uses, including capacitors and transformers.	The U.S. National Academy of Sciences releases a report finding circumstantial evidence linking power-plant emissions of sulphur dioxide with the growing acidification of lakes and streams, the result of acid rain.

"You can only do so much with a Model T."

BRIAN McCLOY, OF THE COUNCIL OF FOREST INDUSTRIES OF BRITISH COLUMBIA; ON WHY COASTAL PULP MILLS FAIL TO MEET CURRENT ENVIRONMENTAL STANDARDS, MARCH 1989

THE ENVIRONMENT AND HEALTH

To what extent have pollution and other environmental damage affected the health of you and your family?

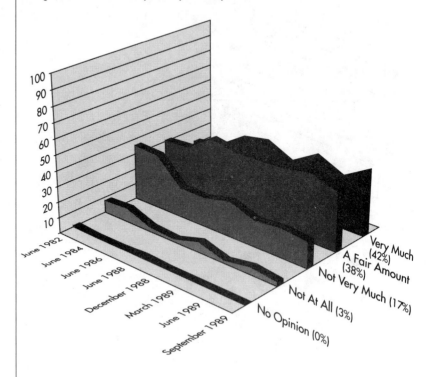

1981	DEC.	1982	JUNE	1983	JAN.
	The European Community bans imports of seal pelts to EC nations from Canada, dealing a crippling blow to the Canadian seal hunt.		Two British scientists working in Antarctica confirm what scientists have long suspected: the existence of a huge gap, hundreds of miles wide, in the earth's ozone layer.		Federal Environment Minister John Roberts says toxic chemicals from U.S. waste dumps near Niagara Falls, N.Y., threaten the drinking water of millions of Canadians.

The question of jobs vs the environment was tougher, but even here the results were amazingly consistent. From March 1980 to June 1989, the number of Canadians who agreed that we must do more to protect our ecology – even if jobs were lost in the process – was never less than 60%. Again, in December 1989, Decima asked what people thought about recycling newspapers, despite the job losses and decline of market-share recycling was likely to cause. A stunning 92% said it was a good idea.

By the end of the decade, the country seemed to hang on the cusp of another recession. Still, as many respondents (23%) said Ottawa's first priority should be to protect the environment as said it should be to ensure a strong economy (23%) or reduce the deficit (22%). The focus on Ottawa was relatively new. In the early 1980s, most Canadians held private industry principally accountable for preventing pollution. It seemed reasonable at the time; those who pollute ought to be the ones to put a stop to it. But reason was consistently disappointed, and by June 1989 a greater number handed that responsibility to the federal government.

In part, this shift acknowledged Ottawa's ability, through legislation, to set – and enforce – firm policies. In part, it recognized that critical environmental problems – air and water pollution, acid rain and ozone depletion – were matters of global concern that a national government was better equipped to address. But it also said something important about private industry – namely, that a declining percentage of Canadians believed that the very industries that were the source of many air- and water-borne pollutants were really committed to the environment. In June 1988, seven out of ten Decima respondents bluntly said the chemical industry did a poor job of protecting the environment. The figures for most other industries were not substantially better.

The absence of trust in industry was reflected in a whole series of questions Decima posed throughout the decade. Asked to cite the most credible source of information on product safety, consumer protection, and other environmental issues, most people said they turned to environmental interest groups; no more than 15% said private industry. When chemical-industry executives or oil- and gas- company spokesmen tried to reassure the country that their products and processes were safe, most Canadians simply didn't believe them. Whatever the business community's

FACTS

What is the world's most polluted mammal? According to some scientists, it is the St. Lawrence beluga whale, which inhabits the befouled St. Lawrence River system.

Number of beluga whales in 1900: 5,000
Number in 1989: 500

Concentrations of PCBs considered dangerous to human health by the federal government: anything greater than 50 parts per million
Concentration found in one shrew southwest of Montreal in 1989: 11,522 parts per million

"All of a sudden, he's being labelled a Lucifer who's trying to poison the population of Canada… when he's not doing anything 95% of all industries don't do."

SHEILA ALEXANDER, WIFE OF KEITH, FORMER PRESIDENT OF JETCO MANUFACTURING LTD., A TORONTO METAL-PLATER, AFTER AN ONTARIO SUPREME COURT JUDGE MADE HIM THE FIRST EXECUTIVE EVER ORDERED TO GO TO JAIL FOR POLLUTION OFFENCES, MAY 1986. ALEXANDER WON ON APPEAL

technical understanding of pollution issues, it was generally judged to be putting its own interests ahead of the country's. And the level of trust was declining as the decade closed. In the eighteen months between June 1988 and December 1989, the percentage of Canadians willing to say the forest industry did a good job of protecting the environment dropped from 60 to 49.

Even in those rare instances where the nation was willing to applaud industries whose environmental performance was considered exemplary, it was suspicious of their motivation. In December 1989, 57% said the packaged-goods industry was doing a good (or very good) job of reducing solid waste by changing product packaging. But 37% said they were doing so because of the profit motive and another 36% said they were only responding to fear of a government or consumer backlash. Only one in five credited the industry with having a genuine commitment to the environment.

As the decade came to an end, Decima uncovered yet another significant shift: in December 1989, 35% said individual Canadians were primarily responsible for protecting the environment; in June 1986, that figure was just 18%. The numbers seemed to suggest that while governments could legislate emission laws and courts could levy fines, only concerted action by ordinary Canadians was likely to bring serious, positive changes in environmental behaviour. In fact, an increasing number of people were inclined to act on that judgement – becoming green activists themselves. In practical terms, activism could mean several things: using recycled goods, not buying aerosol cans and some packaged foods, recycling cans, bottles, and paper, boycotting the products of polluters, purchasing bottled water, using unleaded gas, and, to some extent, avoiding fresh foods grown with the help of pesticides.

Demographically, the green activists were likelier to live in Alberta, British Columbia, or Ontario, have university educations, be middle-aged, earn higher salaries, and work in a technical or professional job. The picture, in fact, was remarkably consistent. Those who cited ecology as a pressing concern were likelier to think environmental quality was declining, likelier to link that decline to health issues, and likelier to change their buying habits and other aspects of their behaviour as a result. They were also likelier – in theory, at least – to endorse fairly Draconian measures aimed at cleaning up the environment.

WHAT IS IT?

DIOXINS AND FURANS: Perhaps the most toxic chemicals in existence, these are by-products of incineration or form as contaminants in the manufacture of chlorophenol herbicides and wood preservatives.

ACID RAIN: When emissions of sulphur dioxide and nitrogen oxides return to earth – in the form of rain, hail, snow, fog, or dust – they acidify rivers, lakes, and streams, killing trees and wildlife, and corroding buildings. In 1980, Canada emitted 4.5 million tonnes of sulphur dioxide into the atmosphere. In 1988, the figure was 3.7 million tonnes. As a result of an agreement with the provinces, Canada is committed to reducing sulphur-dioxide emissions by 1994 to 2.475 million tonnes.

PCBs: Polychlorinated biphenyls are synthetic chemicals consisting of chlorine, carbon, and hydrogen. Stable and fire-resistant, PCBs were in wide use in dozens of consumer and industrial products until they were banned in 1977. To that point, some 635,000 tonnes of PCBs were believed to have been manufactured in North America; 40,000 tonnes are said to have entered Canada.

CFCs: Chlorofluorocarbons are synthetic chemicals consisting of chlorine, fluorine, and carbon molecules. Non-toxic and very stable, CFCs are widely used in air-conditioning systems, aerosol cans, hard and soft foam products, and cleaning solvents. The depletion of the ozone layer, which protects life on earth from ultraviolet radiation, is blamed on CFCs and on halons, their chemical cousins. In the upper atmosphere, the sun's rays quickly break down CFCs, which release chlorine atoms, and halons, which release bromine. Scientists say one chlorine atom can kill about 10,000 ozone molecules; one bromine atom can destroy 100,000.

BIODEGRADABLE: Capable of being broken down, especially into innocuous products by the action of living things. – *Webster's Ninth Collegiate Dictionary*, 1989

FACTS

Amount of nitrogen oxide emissions in Canada in 1985: 1.9 million tonnes Amount produced by automobiles: 912,000 tonnes

Number of tonnes of solid waste disposed of by the city of Toronto in 1967: 500,000 Number of tonnes disposed of in 1988: 3.25 million Percentage increase between 1983 and 1987: 77

"No one retires
from fine
chemicals."

WHAT ARE WE WORRIED ABOUT? (JUNE 1988)

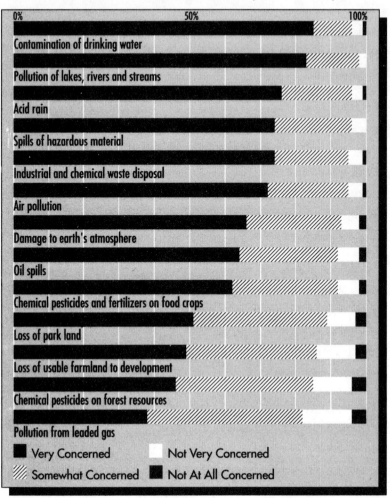

Contamination of drinking water

Pollution of lakes, rivers and streams

Acid rain

Spills of hazardous material

Industrial and chemical waste disposal

Air pollution

Damage to earth's atmosphere

Oil spills

Chemical pesticides and fertilizers on food crops

Loss of park land

Loss of usable farmland to development

Chemical pesticides on forest resources

Pollution from leaded gas

■ Very Concerned   □ Not Very Concerned

▨ Somewhat Concerned   ■ Not At All Concerned

1983 JULY
135,000 litres of soap resins and fatty acids are accidentally dumped in the Spanish River near Espanola, Ont., by E.B. Eddy. Estimated number of fish killed: 50,000. The company calls it a "minor spill."

1984 JAN.
A train wreck near Medicine Hat, Alta., releases toxic gases, forcing the evacuation of 800 residents.

1984 DEC.
Deadly gas is accidentally released from a Union Carbide plant in Bhopal, India. More than 2,500 die. The health of thousands is damaged.

HOW GREAT A RISK? (JUNE 1989)

How much of a health risk to you and your family do the following represent?

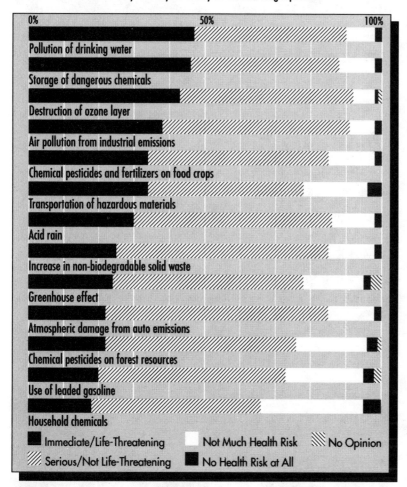

	0%	50%	100%

Pollution of drinking water

Storage of dangerous chemicals

Destruction of ozone layer

Air pollution from industrial emissions

Chemical pesticides and fertilizers on food crops

Transportation of hazardous materials

Acid rain

Increase in non-biodegradable solid waste

Greenhouse effect

Atmospheric damage from auto emissions

Chemical pesticides on forest resources

Use of leaded gasoline

Household chemicals

■ Immediate/Life-Threatening   □ Not Much Health Risk   ▨ No Opinion

▨ Serious/Not Life-Threatening   ■ No Health Risk at All

FACTS

Number of tonnes of packaging used by Canadians in 1988: 6.6 million

Percentage in landfill sites: 82

What's in a landfill site?
Packaging: 30.3%
Nondurables: 25.1%
Yard waste: 20.1%
Durables: 13.6%
Food waste: 8.9%
Miscellaneous: 1.8%

1985 FEB.

Ontario provincial-court judge Vibert Lampkin fines Eagle Disposal Systems $3 million for breaking provincial environmental laws. Status of business when the charges were laid: bankrupt.

1985 AUG.

Manitoba and North Dakota sign agreement on the controversial Garrison River diversion project.

1986 APRIL

A nuclear explosion at Chernobyl, U.S.S.R., sends more than seven tons of radioactive debris into the atmosphere. Tens of thousands are forced to flee their homes. The radiation drifts in clouds across the continent and around the world, contaminating everything it touches.

> "We cannot tell you what the ozone situation will look like in five years and that scares us. We have no predictive power. There may be some unpleasant surprises in store. The only thing I'm sure of is that things can only get worse."
>
> JOE FARMAN, ONE OF TWO BRITISH SCIENTISTS WHO CONFIRMED THE HOLES IN THE OZONE LAYER, DECEMBER 1989

CANCER AND THE OZONE LAYER

Scientists estimate that 3.5% of the earth's ozone layer has already been destroyed by man-made chemicals. At its present rate of destruction, a 50% reduction by the year 2050 is not improbable. In that scenario, doctors estimate that 170,000 people would die from melanoma and another 160 million would develop skin cancer.

WHAT'S IN A GLASS OF WATER?

The city of Toronto's drinking water contains 50 contaminants, 16 of which are cancer-causing. These include arsenic, benzene, cadmium, chloroform, lindane, methylene chloride, chromium, carbon tetrachloride, bromodichlormethane, hexachlorocyclohexane, hexachlorocyclohexane, heptachlor apoxide, nickel, and PCBs. Lindane, to take one example, is present in 1-3 parts per billion. Consuming two litres of water a day means drinking 25-75 billion molecules of lindane a day.

THE VANISHING FOREST   Confidence in the nation's forest industries dropped sharply through the 1980s, reflecting growing anxiety about the relationship between logging and the depletion of the ozone layer.

Consider these figures, derived from a June 1989 Decima poll: 84% would support mandatory recycling programs; 76% would support banning plastic and foam products; 67% would restrict the use of automobiles; and 54% would even ban air conditioners.

The range of our environmental concerns was broad and deep, from leaded gas to loss of parkland, from oil spills to damage to the earth's ozone layer. It even included Canada-U.S. relations. In the spring of 1985, 32% of respondents named acid rain and other ecological problems as the first priority on the Ottawa-Washington agenda; but trade and economic issues, at 40%, were clearly dominant. By the autumn of 1988, however, despite continuing debate about the free-trade agreement, the environment was sharing top billing – the result of acid rain, pollution in the Great Lakes, and other trans-boundary issues.

But in most Decima surveys through the 1980s, contamination of drinking water and industrial and chemical waste dominated the agenda. In some cases, the concern was compounded by our confusion about how to deal with the problem. For example, in September 1989, 48% said incinerating PCBs was either a safe or a very safe way to dispose of these toxic chemicals. But 46% disagreed, contending that burning PCBs was either not very safe or not at all safe. (The scientific community was no less divided.) Despite that ambivalence, fully 75% of respondents thought Canada should build a toxic-waste-disposal facility – and not ship our wastes to other, more hospitable jurisdictions. On the other hand, the Not-In-My-Back-Yard syndrome was powerfully in evidence. No matter how safe the facility might be, no matter what the circumstances, 68% (in 1985) and 56% (in 1989) said they would not want the disposal plant located near their community.

The same attitudes are visible on questions of solid waste. Some 67% say garbage-disposal systems are inadequate now – or will be in the future. But 73% don't want anything to do with new landfill sites in their own community. Doubtless, the root of that sentiment is the presumed linkage between pollution and human health. According to a June 1989 survey, the vast majority of Canadians regard virtually every major environmental issue as either a serious hazard to health – or an immediate threat to life. And when it comes to plastics, for example, 73% of us say the risks of their use outweigh the benefits.

FACTS

Percentage of products made by the packaging industry that are used to wrap or contain food: 60

Annual average wood volume harvested, 1981-85: 153.2 million cubic metres
Estimated annual loss of forests due to fires, disease, and insects: 150-200 million cubic metres
Percentage of tree-harvested land devoted to planting in 1975-80: 18
Percentage in 1980-83: 21
Percentage in 1983-86: 29

THE ENVIRONMENT AND JOBS

We should do more to protect the environment
even if jobs are lost in the process

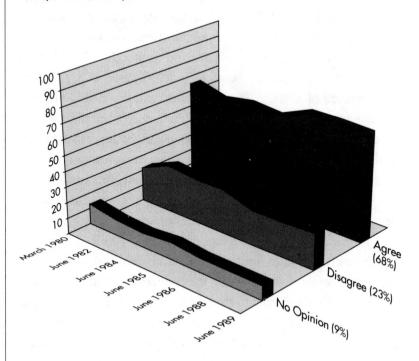

100
90
80
70
60
50
40
30
20
10

March 1980
June 1982
June 1984
June 1985
June 1986
June 1988
June 1989

Agree
(68%)

Disagree (23%)

No Opinion (9%)

1986 DEC.	**1987** FEB.	**1987** SEPT.
An Ontario study says 97 of 147 major industrial plants violated pollution guidelines in 1985. Number of plants omitted from the survey: 11,000.	A Tillsonburg, Ont., electrical dealer is fined $25,000 after dumping three barrels of PCBs in a Hamilton, Ont., shopping centre in 1984. The cost of the cleanup: $95,000. The defence lawyer's argument: her client was "a victim of a transition to a new approach."	Dozens of nations meeting in Montreal agree on measures to protect the ozone layer.

PROFILE: ENVIRONMENTAL PROTECTION VERSUS JOBS (JUNE 1989)

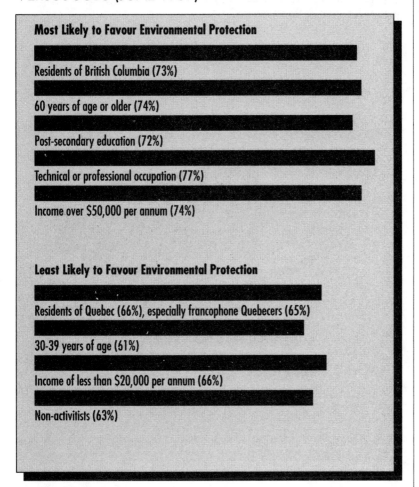

Most Likely to Favour Environmental Protection

Residents of British Columbia (73%)

60 years of age or older (74%)

Post-secondary education (72%)

Technical or professional occupation (77%)

Income over $50,000 per annum (74%)

Least Likely to Favour Environmental Protection

Residents of Quebec (66%), especially francophone Quebecers (65%)

30-39 years of age (61%)

Income of less than $20,000 per annum (66%)

Non-activitists (63%)

FACTS

Frequency with which the Ontario government recommends that certain Great Lakes fish – whose fatty tissues have accumulated PCBs and dioxin – be eaten: not more than once a month

Number of synthetic chemicals currently in use: 70,000
Number added each year: 1,000

1988 JUNE

More than 300 scientists from nations around the world assemble in Toronto to discuss the state of the earth. Global warming, ozone depletion, and acid rain are cited as dominant concerns.

WHO IS RESPONSIBLE?

Who has primary responsibility for preventing
pollution and protecting the environment?

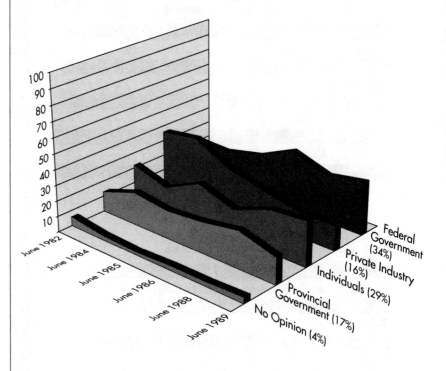

1988 AUG.

A fire in a PCB
storage facility in
Saint Basile-le-Grand,
Quebec, forces
3,300 residents to
flee their homes.
PCBs from the fire
create 15 shipments
of 1,500-3,000
tonnes each.

1988 OCT.

Ottawa pledges
$125 million to clean
up the Great Lakes.

1989 MARCH

A federal study says
83 of Canada's 122
pulp mills exceed
national standards
on dumping toxic
chemicals.

AN INDUSTRY REPORT CARD (JUNE 1988)

Rating corporate performance in protecting the environment

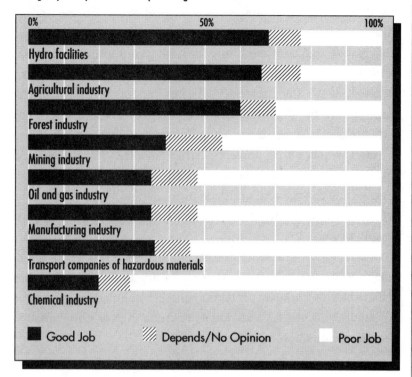

0%	50%	100%

Hydro facilities

Agricultural industry

Forest industry

Mining industry

Oil and gas industry

Manufacturing industry

Transport companies of hazardous materials

Chemical industry

■ Good Job   ▨ Depends/No Opinion   □ Poor Job

HOW GREEN IS BUSINESS?

Business does a good job of protecting the public
from dangerous products and substances

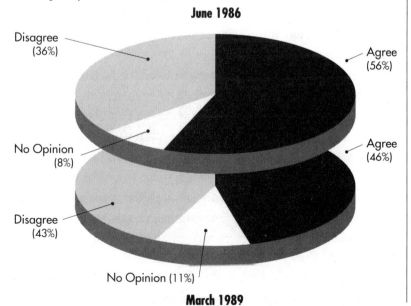

June 1986

Disagree (36%)

Agree (56%)

No Opinion (8%)

Agree (46%)

Disagree (43%)

No Opinion (11%)

March 1989

FACTS

Number of companies in Quebec required by law to report production of toxic waste in 1987: 3,300
Number of companies that complied: fewer than half
Number of tons of toxic waste produced in Quebec in 1987 that could not later be accounted for: 250,000
Its presumed dumping ground: the St. Lawrence River

Estimated number of waste dumps in Canada: 8,784
Number thought to present a health risk: 526

Looking back, it is possible to divide the decade into three quite distinct phases. In the first, Canadians demonstrate increasing interest in and awareness of ecological issues. In the second, awareness becomes concern – and what once might have been merely aesthetic considerations (destruction of forests, acid rain, land-fill problems) are closely linked to health (depletion of the ozone layer to the incidence of skin cancer, to cite just one example). In the third stage, people begin to demand action – by industry and by government – to clean up the environment and to set laws in place that prevent further assaults. But at the same time, they believe that governments are reacting to events, rather than setting the agenda, and recognize that individual Canadians must seize the initiative. Many, if not a majority, are already beginning to do so.

Phase four – in which the green changes now seen as desirable or voluntary are perceived as necessary and mandatory – lies ahead. In this context, protecting the environment is no longer optional behaviour for individuals or industries or governments; it's the sine qua non.

Into the Nineties

Environmental consciousness is the tip of a large iceberg called Quality of Life. Increasingly, Canadians want to improve the quality of their lives – even at the expense of the quantity of their lives.

This is true at both extremes of the income spectrum. At the upper end, the affluent are growing satiated with what has become an unbridled quest for material goods. How many automobiles can a person drive? How many television sets and VCRs can a person watch? The sheer market penetration of consumer products has reached a level where the population is looking for something more. The person who can afford anything begins to want different things: a better education for his children, a longer vacation, or cooking classes. For different reasons, people at the lower end of the income spectrum have arrived at exactly the same place. It's not that they're satiated with material possessions; they're fatigued with the quest itself. Knowing that a BMW is forever out of reach, they confront desires that are at once more basic and

WHAT ARE WE DOING ABOUT IT?

What steps are you and your family taking
to protect the environment?

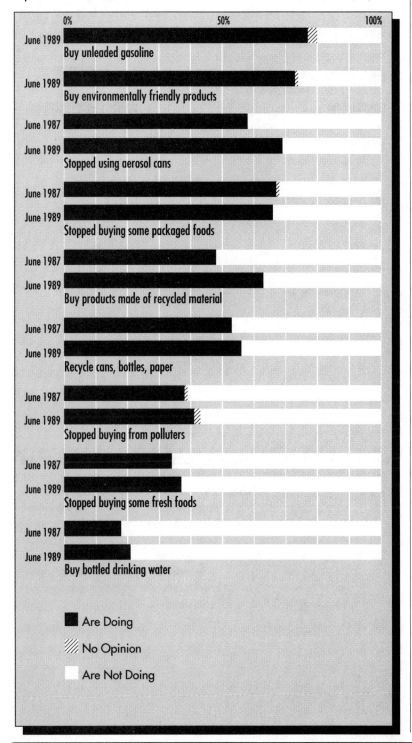

| | 0% | 50% | 100% |

June 1989 Buy unleaded gasoline

June 1989 Buy environmentally friendly products

June 1987
June 1989 Stopped using aerosol cans

June 1987
June 1989 Stopped buying some packaged foods

June 1987
June 1989 Buy products made of recycled material

June 1987
June 1989 Recycle cans, bottles, paper

June 1987
June 1989 Stopped buying from polluters

June 1987
June 1989 Stopped buying some fresh foods

June 1987
June 1989 Buy bottled drinking water

■ Are Doing

▨ No Opinion

☐ Are Not Doing

FACTS

Percentage of
Canada's hazardous
wastes generated
within the Great
Lakes basin: 41

Level of the carcino-
genic compound
trihalomethane
allowed in Canadian
drinking water; 350
parts per billion
Level allowed in the
United States: 100
parts per billion
Cancer incidence
projected by the
Canadian level: 184
cases per 100,000
population

Number of Americans
who participated in
the first Earth Day,
April 22, 1970:
20 million
Number of citizens
around the world
who celebrated Earth
Day, 1990: an esti-
mated half billion

DRASTIC MEASURES (JUNE 1989)

Would you support the following measures
to protect the environment?

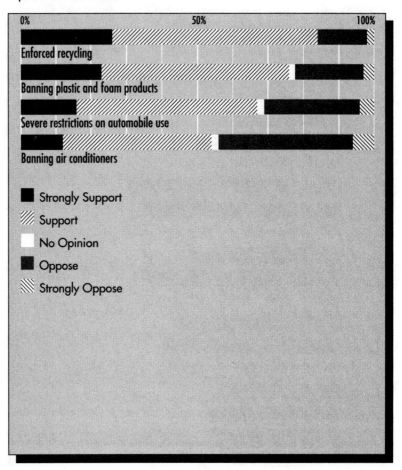

0%	50%	100%

Enforced recycling

Banning plastic and foam products

Severe restrictions on automobile use

Banning air conditioners

■ Strongly Support

▨ Support

□ No Opinion

■ Oppose

▨ Strongly Oppose

1989 MARCH

The tanker Exxon Valdez runs aground off the coast of Alaska, emptying 250,000 barrels of crude oil into Prince William Sound.

1989 APRIL

An environmental licence granted to the Rafferty-Alameda Dam project in southern Saskatchewan is revoked by the Federal Court of Canada.

1989 AUG.

The Saskatchewan dam project gets new life after Environment Minister Lucien Bouchard gives his approval.

TOXIC WASTE

Would you support the establishment of a facility for
the disposal of toxic waste produced in Canada?

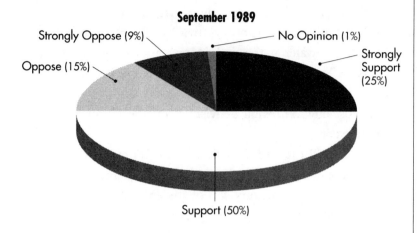

September 1989

Strongly Oppose (9%) — No Opinion (1%)

Oppose (15%) — Strongly Support (25%)

Support (50%)

NOT IN OUR BACKYARD

No matter what the circumstance or how safe they said it was, I am unwilling
to have a hazardous waste disposal site located near my community

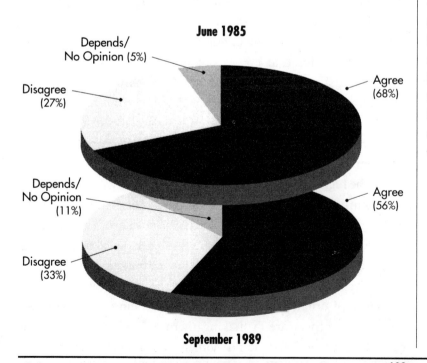

June 1985

Depends/No Opinion (5%)

Disagree (27%)

Agree (68%)

Depends/No Opinion (11%)

Agree (56%)

Disagree (33%)

September 1989

FACTS

**Number of Canadian
homes drinking bot-
tled water or water
purified in home
treatment systems:
1 in 6
Number doing so
in Montreal: 1 in 3
Estimated 1980 sales
of bottled water:
$30 million
Estimated 1989 sales
of bottled water:
$175 million**

**Number of brands of
spring water found
by Canadian Con-
sumer Magazine in
a 1986 survey to
contain more barium
– a toxic metallic
element – than
federal guidelines
recommend: 4 of 15
Number of provinces
that have passed
legislation regulating
contents of bottled
water: 1 – Quebec**

more urgent: fixing the health-care system, the education system, the environment.

There is also a growing sense of involuntary exposure to risk. Canadians sense things happening that they can't control. The most frightening risks are always invisible: things we ingest, things that are in the water, in the air. It is conventional wisdom that these soft issues loom large only in times of prosperity. As economic anxiety increases, they typically fade away. But as we move into the 1990s, environmental activism is on the rise together with economic concern.

What will the decade look like, environmentally? The first phenomenon will be the development of a popular lexicon. It's happening already. Elementary-school students can precisely define what chlorofluorocarbons are. Increasingly, people understand that there are environmental risks in their own homes – that it isn't safe to let the oilpan seep into the asphalt. Our ecological knowledge base is rapidly expanding, and with it the vocabulary of environmental hazards.

Second, concern will shift to the local level. Canadians will continue to worry about acid rain and global warming, but they will be more vigilant about their own houses. Recycling programs will increase exponentially. People will be taught how to dispose of household toxins and chemicals. The bottled-water and water-purification industries will continue to thrive. In fact, people will look at the water that comes out of their taps as suitable for washing dishes, watering plants, and perhaps showering – mouths closed. They certainly won't permit their children to drink it. A whole range of products – paints and glues and solvents and other household items – may disappear, proven to be environmentally hazardous.

The highest levels of activism and militancy will take place in the community, as Canadians try to control their environment by making it smaller. But it will no longer be sufficient to voice concern; people will want solutions. As a result, there will be a growing fascination with – and demand for – environmental technology.

The demand for action will be accompanied by an increasing sense of unfairness. People will resent being asked to make sacrifices if others aren't making them as well. A more severe manifestation of the same phenomenon will be a growing sense

ENVIRONMENTALLY UNFRIENDLY   Toxic industrial wastes were increasingly alarming to Canadians in the 1980s as they came to realize that anything that threatened the natural world also threatened their health.

1989 AUG.

Quebec tries to ship PCBs from Saint-Basile-le-Grand to Liverpool, but the ship is turned back. Most of the waste remains in storage in Saint-Basile.

1989 NOV.

Some 440,000 gallons of radioactive water are spilled at a government-owned uranium mine in northern Saskatchewan because of a faulty valve.

1989 DEC.

The Federal Court orders Lucien Bouchard to carry out a full environmental review of the Saskatchewan Rafferty-Alameda dam or the project will lose its licence.

of deprivation. Canadians will not enjoy being told that gas bar-
becues are illegal, that air conditioning may be used only twice a
week, that they can't drive their cars unless someone else is in
them. Eventually, governments will restrict driving on freeways in
rush hour to cars carrying four people. At that point, someone will
insist that Canadians have electric cars. Of course, the advocate of
electric cars is going to win ninety-nine times out of a hundred over
the bureaucrat who imposes limits.

The thrust of public policy, as we enter the 1990s, is toward
life-style and behavioural change, rather than technological
change. But this is a recipe for grief in the political process – first,
because technological expectations will outstrip their availability;
and second, because pressure will mount on government to create
an industrial strategy that exploits the talent in public and private
laboratories.

For Canadians, the pursuit of environmental improvement
may become a search for the Holy Grail. The environment is
built into our frame of reference. We aren't as powerful as
Americans, but we think we're better. The quality of our environment, our pristine lakes and rivers, are evidence of that supposed superiority. As a result, degrading the environment not
only threatens our wellbeing, it also threatens our sense of who
we are. Just as Canadians in the 1950s took great pride in the
nation's role as peacekeepers in the Middle East, so we will have
an opportunity in the 1990s to become world leaders in environmental technology.

But that's the rosy scenario, in which interests merge, and
policy-makers in government and industry understand that they
must head off an environmental crisis. If they don't, if public policy
trails public opinion, a frustrated population will focus on fairness
and deprivation. At that point, environmental issues will become
more political – and controversial. The population will become
more cynical, and the business community, in particular, could
face trouble. Its instinct will be to play the public-relations game.
But one example that contradicts its claims – no matter how vocal
the claims or how many examples it cites to support them – will
destroy its credibility. People will conclude that business is lying.
In the 1990s, no-one will be able to play public-relations games
with the environment.

In a crisis scenario, cynicism will be accompanied by a growing disbelief in the efficacy of traditional institutions to deal with the environment. In fact, the public will see government and business as principal contributors to the problem. A third party may well emerge, promising solutions. For the first time in two decades, our universities may become relevant. Or we may see the rise of grass-roots entrepreneurship.

There will be marches and demonstrations, of course, but the most effective protests in the 1990s will take place at the cash register. The threat of product boycotts is powerful and real. Until recently, for example, Tide refused to make a phosphate-free detergent. When Loblaw introduced one, Tide had a product on the shelves almost the next week. Corporations cannot afford to ignore this trend. People are cynical. For forty years, they've been told that detergents – and many other products – are "new" and "improved," but they don't believe it any more. What they believe is that for all practical purposes most products cost the same and are the same. As a result, more consumers will make buying decisions based on how much manufacturers donate to, say, leukemia research, or to environmental causes – boycotting those that ignore such issues.

More knowledgeable about the problems and impatient for solutions, some Canadians will simply run away. The exodus from the cities will be driven not only by concern about drugs and crime, but by the environment. Traffic jams are frustrating and unproductive, but they also raise levels of carbon monoxide. In the absence of technological solutions, an increasing number of people will be tempted to create their own, by leaving the problem behind.

FACTS

Canada produces more waste per person than any other nation in the world. A federal study found that Canadians generate 1.8 kg per person per day, compared to 1.63 kg for Americans.

Total number of employees in the plastics industry in Canada in 1985: 38,182
Value of plastics manufacturing in 1980: $2.2 billion
In 1985: $4.4 billion

PH factor of normal rainfall: 5.6
PH factor of the average rainstorm in North America: 4-4.5
(i.e. the rain is at least ten times as acidic as a normal shower)

WEALTH AND WELFARE

CHAPTER 6

"When there is an income tax, the just man will pay more and the unjust less on the same amount of income."

PLATO, *THE REPUBLIC*

"In general, the art of government consists in taking as much money as possible from one class of citizens to give it to the other."

VOLTAIRE, 1764

"There can be no freedom or beauty about a home life that depends on borrowing and debt."

IBSEN, *A DOLL'S HOUSE*, 1879

IN ONE FORM OR ANOTHER, THE SUBJECT OF MONEY PREOCCUPIED Canadians in the 1980s. From inflation to recession, tax reform to free trade, the federal deficit to interest rates, unemployment to the Goods and Services Tax, financial and economic issues dominated the national agenda. The ranking changed, depending on circumstances, but the slate of national grievances at the end of the decade looked very much as it had at the beginning.

The seminal event was the recession of 1981-82, the worst period of economic duress since the Great Depression of the 1930s. The recession shaped Canadian opinion and behaviour for the entire decade and beyond, casting its dark shadow over economic hopes and fears, and affecting attitudes to saving and spending, both by individuals and by governments.

Intimations of recession were already apparent in Decima

DECADE OF GREED   On Friday, October 23, 1987, floor traders at the
Toronto Stock Exchange celebrated the close of the worst week in the market's
history, an event that signalled the end of an era of windfall profits.

"Anyone who expects any major changes from these sessions must be smoking something."

DOUGLAS PETERS, CHIEF ECONOMIST OF THE TORONTO DOMINION BANK, DURING THE JUNE 1988 GROUP OF SEVEN ECONOMIC SUMMIT

surveys in 1980. Almost three-quarters of respondents described the performance of the economy as only fair or poor. And four in ten respondents predicted that the economy would be in worse condition by 1985. The central concern was inflation, an unwanted remnant of the 1970s. In the summer of 1981, more people (36%) called inflation the most serious problem facing the nation than all other economic issues combined. And 65% said inflation had forced changes in life style – most noticeably the ability to save. In fact, inflation eroded real income so palpably that Canadians began to question the assumption that had governed the country since the Second World War – that progress is the norm.

But as the leading source of pessimism, inflation soon had competition. By December of 1981, rising interest rates and the general health of the economy were cited by an increasing number of Canadians as the country's most serious problem. In fact, as job layoffs mounted and the cost of home mortgages soared, many of us were unable to identify the single most problematic economic issue: all were equally troubling. The confusion – and the stress – affected our self-confidence. By 1981, roughly six out of ten believed that contemporary problems were too complicated even to understand, and that the average person lacked the power to change the course of events.

Still, Canadians clung to the notion that the country could solve its economic problems – collectively, if not individually. In 1981, a clear majority stubbornly refused to accept the suggestion that "nothing could be done about inflation; it was something we simply had to learn to live with." We were convinced that Ottawa could find solutions, just as it had in the past. Government already played a huge role in our economic life, a role most of us believed beneficial. Indeed, it was support for an expanded federal presence that led, in 1980, to the National Energy Program.

But the recession's grim numbers – interest rates at 21%, unemployment at 11% – soon undermined this conviction. In June of 1982, 66% said Canada's economic performance was poor and 61% thought our personal prospects were worse than they had been several years earlier. Our faith in government was shattered. While acknowledging the increased role of government in economic affairs, a remarkable 71% of Canadians said the federal intervention hampered economic growth; 62% even thought it had

THE CONFUSION FACTOR

Today's problems are so complicated,
I can't understand what's going on

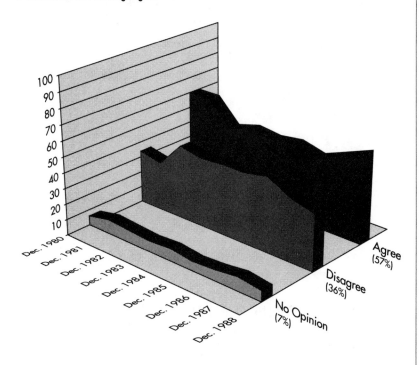

100
90
80
70
60
50
40
30
20
10

Dec. 1980
Dec. 1981
Dec. 1982
Dec. 1983
Dec. 1984
Dec. 1985
Dec. 1986
Dec. 1987
Dec. 1988

Agree
(57%)

Disagree
(36%)

No Opinion
(7%)

FACTS

Net worth of the average Canadian in December 1987: $77,960
Net worth in 1986: $72,000
The definition of net worth: the total of all Canadian assets, less foreign liabilities, divided by 26 million

Net worth of all Canadians in 1980: $1.14 trillion
Net worth of all Canadians in 1988: $1.99 trillion

Average annual increase in union wage settlements from 1984-88: 4.2%
Average wage settlement in 1989: 5.2%
Average increase in Consumer Price Index from 1984-88: 4.2%
Increase in Consumer Price Index in 1989: 5.3%

1980 OCT.
The federal Liberal government introduces a budget projecting the deficit at $14 billion. Expenditures rise 13%.

1980 NOV.
Canadian chartered banks raise the prime rate to 13.25% from 12.75%.

1980 DEC.
One-year mortgage rates hit 16%.

THROUGH THE EIGHTIES

UNEMPLOYMENT		INFLATION*	
1980:	7.5%	1980:	10.2%
1981:	7.5%	1981:	12.5%
1982:	11.0%	1982:	10.8%
1983:	11.9%	1983:	5.8%
1984:	11.3%	1984:	4.4%
1985:	10.5%	1985:	3.9%
1986:	9.6%	1986:	4.2%
1987:	8.9%	1987:	4.4%
1988:	7.8%	1988:	4.1%
1989:	7.5%	1989:	5.3%

* As measured by changes in the Consumer Price Index

NET INTEREST ON THE PUBLIC DEBT

In 1940: $114.4 million

In 1950: $348.3 million

In 1960: $495.9 million

In 1970: $815.9 million

In 1980: $4.9 billion

In 1988: $24.3 billion

FEDERAL BUDGET DEFICITS

1980-81:	$13.5 billion
1981-82:	$14.9 billion
1982-83:	$27.8 billion
1983-84:	$32.4 billion
1984-85:	$38.3 billion
1985-86:	$34.4 billion
1986-87:	$30.6 billion
1987-88:	$28.1 billion
1988-89:	$28.7 billion
1989-90:	$30.5 billion
1990-91:	$28.5 billion*

* projected

a negative impact on our quality of life; and only 47% believed any longer that Ottawa possessed some fiscal potion that could either cure the country's economic diseases or allow us to fulfil our potential. This marked a fundamental shift in Canadian attitudes. Wherever the answers now lay, it was certainly not in Ottawa.

Looking back, it is clear that the recession destroyed what was left of Canadian belief in the future-is-progress ethos. It is equally clear why. In theory, we thought governments capable of solving problems; experience showed they were not. In the abstract, we regarded Canada as the best place in the world in which to live; in reality, only 25% were happy with the direction the country was taking. In principle, we endorsed the idea that hard work was all that was needed to reach one's goals; in fact, 67% feared that at least one family member would be out of work in the immediate future. The recession, in short, completely and utterly contradicted our traditional values. It was not that those values were obsolete, but that the traditional means of pursuing them were no longer viable. The old remedies had somehow lost potency. New ones were needed – and Canadians would spend much of the rest of the decade looking for them.

If it is possible to mark the precise nadir of the recession, at least in terms of Canadian opinion, it may have been June of 1982. After that date, an increasing number of us voiced confidence in the future – both for the country and ourselves. Economically, we had touched bottom. More importantly, we had survived. Indeed, coping with the harsh consequences of unemployment and bankruptcy revived our faith in our own problem-solving abilities. Significantly, however, the decline in interest rates and the easing of inflation did not restore our trust in government.

The most visible index of doubt was unemployment, which continued to rise into 1983. Again, large majorities of Canadians challenged the ability of government to deal with economic problems. Instead, we were increasingly inclined to turn to private enterprise for solutions. By the summer of 1983, the private sector was rated more capable than government of creating new jobs, protecting existing ones, serving broad economic interests, and promoting growth. And so it remained for the entire decade.

The recession left other scars as well. Even as the economy gathered steam, Canadians voiced caution, fearing a resurgence of

FACTS

Number of Canadians filing tax returns in 1986: 16 million
Number taken to court for tax evasion: 130
Number convicted: 128
Number jailed: 4

Average amount of tax paid by someone earning $45,000-$50,000 a year in 1980: $9,209
Average amount paid in 1989: $10,170

Amount of personal income tax paid by residents of Quebec on earnings of $50,000 in 1988: $15,700
Next highest amount: $14,000, in Newfoundland

Number of business failures in 1980: 27,620
Number in 1989: 37,866

"There is only so much plonk that I am prepared to drink for my country."

MORDECAI RICHLER, TESTIFYING IN FAVOUR OF THE FREE-TRADE AGREEMENT BEFORE A PARLIAMENTARY COMMITTEE, OCTOBER 1987

inflation and interest rates. In December 1983, a majority of us were still unwilling even to contemplate making a major purchase in the next six months. And when asked what we would do with a $10,000 windfall, 81% said we would pay off debts, invest in stocks or a business, or simply save it. The recession had taught us not only how to tighten our belts; it had taught us that the economy was a fickle engine, prone to breakdown – and we had best be prepared for the consequences.

In part, our concern was a function of international developments, of which Canadians were increasingly aware. The U.S. invasion of Grenada, Britain's war with Argentina in the Falkland Islands, the mounting debate over new NATO nuclear-missile deployments in Europe: these events inevitably raised global tensions. In an uncertain world, economic security seemed an oxymoron. Not surprisingly, Canadians expressed pessimism about both the short- and long-term economic future. By the middle of 1984, large majorities expected interest rates, inflation, and unemployment to rise within six months. Most of us, in fact, doubted that a recovery of any sort was under way. And those who did see signs of economic improvement regarded it as merely temporary.

In that context, the election of Brian Mulroney's Conservative government in September 1984 may have been inevitable. During the campaign, the Tories had decried the status quo, advocating non-interventionist policies that would be unapologetically free-market and pro-business. The theme struck a resonant chord, and the period following the election was characterized by great expectations on several important fronts – general economic prospects, job creation, tax restraint, inflation reduction, government spending. Four out of five Canadians also believed that closer economic ties with the United States would benefit the country economically, and almost seven out of ten maintained that the potential gains outweighed the risk to Canada's political and economic independence.

The optimism did not last long, and concern about Canada's long-term economic health continued to run at high levels. In part, this reflected the unevenness of economic recovery. Several demographic and regional groups lagged, notably older and lower-income Canadians, especially in the West. At one point, 72% of Newfoundlanders cited unemployment as the country's most

FREE TRADE: PRO OR CON

Do you oppose or favour entering into a free-trade agreement with the United States?

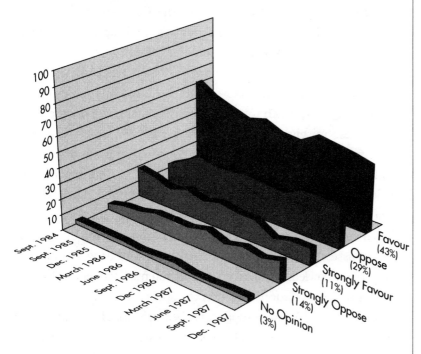

FACTS

Percentage of tax filers earning between $15,000 and $25,000 in 1986: 52
Percentage earning $25,001-$35,000: 29
Percentage earning $35,001-$50,000: 15
Percentage earning $50,001-$75,000: 5
Percentage earning $75,001-$100,000: 1
Percentage earning more than $100,000: 1

City with highest per capita income in 1988: Toronto ($19,138)
City with lowest: Charlottetown ($12,178)
Canadian average: $14,753

City with highest average household income in 1988: Toronto ($53,987)
City with lowest: Victoria ($34,726)
Canadian average: $40,889

1981 JUNE
Statistics Canada reports a 1.5% increase in the Consumer Price Index, bringing annual inflation to a record 12.8%.

1981 JULY
The Bank of Canada lending rate hits 20.54%.

1981 NOV.
Another federal budget, raising revenues, projects a deficit of $10.5 billion.

important issue; in Ontario, the figure was only 26%. In a nation governed by a belief in fairness, an economy that thrived in one region and chronically stumbled in another was too visible a stain.

Another source of concern was the Conservative budget of May 1985, which failed – in the public's mind at least – to meet demands for equitable tax and economic reform. Instead, it seemed to confirm that hard work and merit were no longer sufficient guarantors of success. In fact, four out of five Canadians subscribed to the notion that the rich were growing richer, and the poor, poorer.

These misgivings were underscored by the developing furor over free trade. The debate itself was not new, but it was different in kind from other issues Canadians had confronted. The impact of inflation and interest rates were felt in every paycheque. The proposal to negotiate a free-trade agreement with Washington was, by definition, a voyage into unknown territory, an economic roll of the dice. And in assessing the costs and benefits, most of us would need to rely on the knowledge and experience of potential winners and losers.

As the negotiations began in the spring of 1986, most Canadians – 7 out of 10 – were supportive, believing that free trade would strengthen the economy and create jobs. But ensuing polls demonstrated that this support was marshmallow-soft. Within a year, only 58% still favoured an agreement, 50% doubted it would benefit the economy, and 51% said the risk to Canadian independence outweighed any potential gains. In part, the decline simply reflected the race to win the public policy debate: opponents of free trade were quicker off the mark than advocates, raising the spectre of industry closures, job layoffs, and the loss of sovereignty. But in part the turnabout reflected our chronic uncertainty about the future.

The signing of the draft free-trade agreement (FTA) in October 1987 only heightened anxiety. That December, 21% said the FTA was a problem facing Canada. (Only 6% had the previous June.) Only 44% backed the principle of free trade itself – the lowest level of the decade. And for the first time no majority could be mustered in support of the notion that free trade would benefit the economy. In fact, most Canadians thought the Americans had won the upper hand on those aspects of the agreement affecting energy and investment. As a result, 77% concluded that a better deal might have been struck.

The great divide in public opinion dominated the 1988

federal election. But neither the pro-free-trade Conservatives nor the anti-free-trade Liberals and New Democrats gained much ground; the percentages in favour and opposed were roughly the same in December as they had been in March, with a slim majority endorsing the accord. (The Tories won a majority re-election, capturing 169 of 295 seats in Parliament and 43% of the popular vote.) In the post-mortems that followed the agreement's first anniversary, most Canadians said free trade had not affected personal wellbeing. But we were decidedly less sanguine about its impact on the economy generally; only 19% noticed any benefit. Indeed, in a December 1989 poll, nearly half the country (48%) thought Ottawa should invoke the clause that allowed either party to opt out with six months' notice.

Ironically, the global stock-market crash of October 1987 seemed to have only a minimal impact on public confidence. Fewer Canadians were prepared to invest in the stock market after October 19, 1987, but 53% said we had been largely or completely unaffected by its decline. In fact, a huge majority (72%) voiced satisfaction with our current financial circumstances and 54% said "personal prospects" were better now than they had been four or five years earlier. Still, most people considered December of 1987 "a bad time for making a major purchase" – with or without credit. And a new and troubling gap in public opinion had emerged: for the first time in the decade, Canadians felt more confident about the current situation than they did about the future.

The implications were stunning. Even in good times, the country seemed to be nagged by a growing sense that prosperity was a mirage, that the events that influenced our economic lives were not only beyond our control, but beyond our understanding. That reflexive pessimism was present even as unemployment, inflation, and interest rates dropped to record lows. By 1989, Decima surveys showed a steep decline in assessments of the economy. The present was deteriorating, the polls said; the future would be worse. Two-thirds forecast a recession. Consumer confidence was plummeting. And 43% – offered a hypothetical $10,000 windfall said it would be used to reduce debt (per-capita debt levels were at a ten-year high). The downturn was coming – and memories of the recession were all too vivid.

FACTS

Average annual family income in 1980: $28,006 In 1987: $43,604

Percentage of families earning more than $75,000 in 1986: 7.9 Percentage earning less than $20,000: 21.5

Income of average two-parent family with one worker in 1980: $37,449 Income of same family in 1988 (adjusted for inflation): $37,351

Percentage of family income derived from employment earnings in 1988: 81.6 Percentage derived from investment: 4.7 From government transfer payments: 10 From other sources: 3.7

"We can't get enough Jags. We have more customers than cars. When guys are plunking down this much money, buying a car is a real experience. They like to wheel and deal. They like how we do it, like how we relieve them of vast sums of money."

STEVEN KASTNER, GENERAL MANAGER OF A TORONTO JAGUAR AND ROLLS-ROYCE DEALERSHIP, 1986

"How much money does a person need?"

STEPHEN SANDER, A SIKH BUSINESS-MAN IN VANCOUVER WHO ARRIVED IN CANADA FROM INDIA IN 1960. IN DECEMBER 1989, HE ANNOUNCED HE WAS SETTING UP A CHARITABLE FOUN-DATION TO DISTRIBUTE THE REVENUES FROM HIS 123 APARTMENT BUILDINGS TO THE HOMELESS, THE SICK, AND THE AGED

WHAT WOULD YOU DO WITH $10,000?

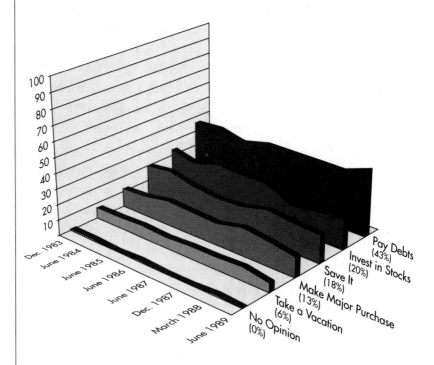

WHAT IS IT?

THE POVERTY LINE: According to Statistics Canada, the poverty line — otherwise known as the low-income cut-off — is drawn where families live in straitened circumstances, spending more than 58.5% of pre-tax income on food, clothing, and shelter. In 1987, an estimated 3.5 million Canadians lived below the line, about one in every seven. Newfoundland recorded the highest percentage of poor — 20.8. Ontario recorded the lowest — 10.3.

RECESSION: According to economists, a recession is two consecutive quarters — six months — of negative growth in a country's real gross national product.

DISPOSABLE INCOME: The term used by economists and financial experts to describe what is left to consumers after taxes.

PERSONAL DEBT

Are you more or less in debt now
than you were 6 months ago?

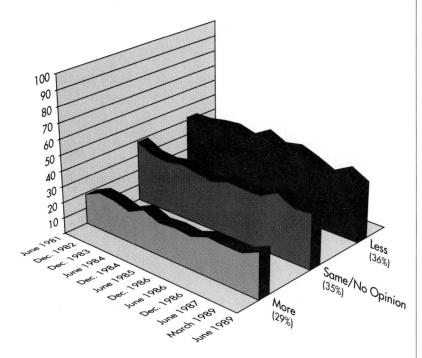

FACTS

**Percentage of all
income earned by
top 20% of income
earners (more
than $64,800) in
1988: 39.2
Percentage of all
income earned by
bottom 20% of
income earners (less
than $22,006): 6.5**

**Average income in
1988 of families
headed by university
graduates: $67,071**

**Average income of
families in Ontario
in 1988: $52,764
Of families in Prince
Edward Island:
$34,535**

**Number of cars pur-
chased by Canadians
in 1982: 718,000
Number purchased in
1985: 1,135,000**

**Total consumer debt
in 1981: $46 billion
Total in 1989:
$92.6 billion
Percentage decrease
in borrowing from
1988: 13**

1982 ## FEB.

Cadillac Fairview, one
of the country's largest
real-estate companies,
announces it is getting
out of the land and
housing business. It
puts 56% of its prop-
erties up for sale.

1982 ## MARCH

Statistics Canada
reports that Canada
has entered a reces-
sion. The following
month the unemploy-
ment rate hits 13.6%
– 1.6 million Canadi-
ans – its highest
level in 40 years.

1982 ## JUNE

Another federal
budget limits wage
increases in the
public service to 6%
and calls for a deficit
of $19.6 billion.

"It's a hell of a time to be a union leader, or any other type of leader for that matter."

DONALD NICHOLSON, PRESIDENT OF THE 36,000 MEMBER CANADIAN BROTHERHOOD OF RAILWAY, TRANSPORT AND GENERAL WORKERS, JUNE 1982

"A kitchen in a large house. What do you think it'd cost? How does $100,000 sound to you? A bathroom is $50,000."

JACK WINSTON, AN INTERIOR DESIGNER, ON THE NEW AFFLUENCE OF TORONTO, 1986

By June 1989, there were two new sources of concern – the federal deficit and taxation. Even as early as 1982, Canadians had endorsed deficit reduction, believing it would spur the economy. But for most of us, cutting the debt meant eliminating government waste and inefficiency – not raising taxes or trimming social programs. Indeed, large numbers of Canadians voiced firm opposition to using sales- or income-tax increases to slash the deficit, and to cutting government spending on child care, regional-development incentives, or future energy megaprojects. That waste and inefficiency were bit players in the deficit drama did not matter; 80% thought they were the leads. Only 5% said the deficit should be blamed on insufficient tax revenues, while 14% fingered federal program spending. And an overwhelming majority maintained that ordinary Canadians shouldered a disproportionate share of the sacrifices needed to cut the federal debt.

The Conservative budget in April 1989 hardened attitudes. Less than one in four respondents believed its reforms would yield a fairer system. The resistance to the budget grew directly from our perception of the problem: government created the dragon; government must slay it. Raising the tax burden on average Canadians was not the answer; 53% endorsed the proposition that Ottawa should be able to cut the deficit without wounding the taxpayer.

Committed to fairness, the country welcomed tax reform, but the results drew mixed reviews. Closing tax loopholes was popular, as was reducing taxes for low-income earners, cutting personal tax rates and eliminating tax shelters. But in June 1987, 70% opposed broadening the sales-tax base – the basic thrust of the proposed Goods and Services Tax (GST), scheduled to take effect in January 1991. And only four in ten Canadians surveyed concluded that the total tax-reform package would produce a fairer tax system. Predictably, the unveiling of the GST proposal in April 1989 was greeted by a chorus of contempt. Most Canadians regarded it as a blatant tax grab, and more than 60% said it would make the tax system less fair. By September, virtually 8 in 10 were opposed to the new levy – even while recognizing that it was aimed at cutting the deficit and making our manufactured goods more competitive. The purity of the motives was irrelevant; 44% said GST revenues would be wasted by government mismanagement and excess.

MOOD SWINGS

Do you think the economy will be better or worse in the next 4 or 5 years?

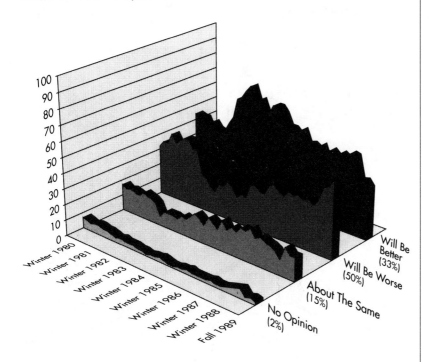

FACTS

Amount Canadian homeowners owed in mortgages to banks, trust and loans, life insurers, credit unions and pension funds in 1980: $84.9 billion Amount they owed in 1988: $184.4 billion

Percentage of income devoted to servicing mortgage and taxes of the average home in 1983: 34.3 Percentage in 1989: 37.8

Percentage of disposable income saved by Canadians in 1981: 15.42 Percentage in 1982: 17.8 Percentage in 1985: 13.6 Percentage in 1988: 9.2 Percentage in 1989: 10.2

The federal minimum wage in 1970: $1.65 an hour In 1980: $3.25 In 1989: $4.00

1982 OCT.

The Finance Minister, Marc Lalonde, issues an economic statement, forecasting a budget deficit of $23.6 billion.

1984 JAN.

Stuart and Lillian Kelly become the continent's largest-ever lottery winners, holding a winning Lotto 6-49 ticket worth $13.8 million.

1984 FEB.

The Liberals table another budget, forecasting a budget deficit of $31.5 billion.

"Would you prefer to locate in the United States, and ship ninety percent of your sales to Camden, New Jersey, and ten percent to Bramalea, or locate in Bramalea and ship ninety percent all the way to Camden?"

ERIC KIERANS, FORMER FEDERAL MINISTER OF COMMUNICATIONS, ON THE IMPACT OF THE FREE-TRADE AGREEMENT ON CANADA'S MANUFACTURING SECTOR, 1988

CANADA'S MOST IMPORTANT ECONOMIC PROBLEMS

What is the most important problem facing Canada today?

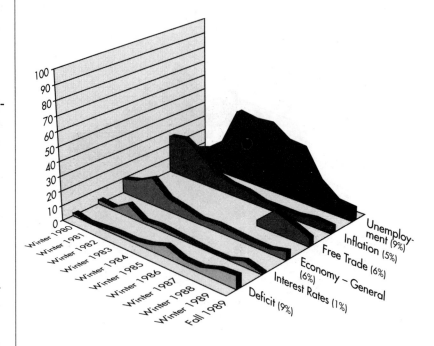

1985 MAY
The first budget introduced by Conservative Finance Minister Michael Wilson calls for the de-indexation of old-age security and family-allowance benefits, fuelling a storm of protest.

1985 AUG.
The Macdonald Royal Commission on Canada's economic prospects concludes that a free-trade agreement with the United States would be neither a panacea nor a disaster. Saying that it requires a leap of faith, the Commission recommends that it be pursued.

1987 OCT.
After more than a year of negotiation, Ottawa and Washington sign a draft treaty on free trade aimed at dismantling all barriers to cross-border trade over a ten-year period. The agreement is formally signed by Prime Minister Brian Mulroney and U.S. President Ronald Reagan in January, 1988.

SHOULD THE GOVERNMENT BE IN BUSINESS?

Would an increase in government involvement in business
help or hinder Canada's economic potential?

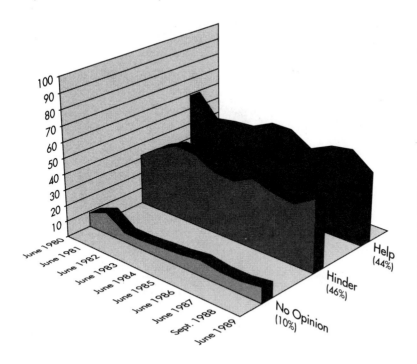

FACTS

**Average cost of a
domestic automobile
in 1983: $11,000
Average cost in
1989: $15,800
Average cost of an
imported automobile
in 1983: $10,500
Average cost in
1989: $18,000**

**Income category into
which largest percent-
age of families living
in Winnipeg fell in
1986: $20,000-
$24,999 (10.1%)
In Calgary:
$35,000-$39,999
(10.2%)
In Vancouver:
$40,000-$44,999
(10.7%)
In Toronto:
$75,000+ (16.0%)**

VITAL STATISTICS

Canada's current-account balance in 1977: $–4.4 billion

Japan's current-account balance in 1977: $11.6 billion

Canada's current-account balance in 1987: $–9.6 billion

Japan's current-account balance in 1987: $115.4 billion

Percentage share of Canada's gross domestic product claimed by
Ontario and Quebec in 1982: 59.8

Percentage held by those provinces in 1989: 65.1

Quebec's share in 1982: 23.1%

Its share in 1989: 23.6%

Alberta's share in 1982: 14.2%

Its share in 1989: 10.4%

"Next to self-flagellation, probably the most horrific autopunishment known to man would be to voluntarily attend a special seminar on the macro-economic effects of the goods and services tax."

TERENCE CORCORAN, *GLOBE AND MAIL* COLUMNIST, DECEMBER 1989

ASSESSING THE BUDGET

In general, how satisfied are you with the federal budget?

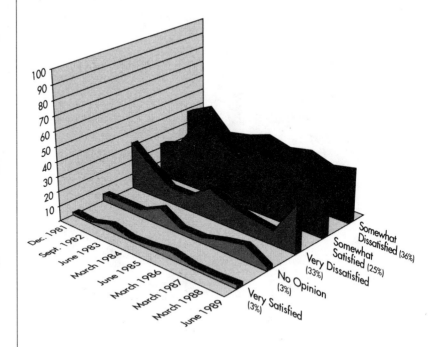

1987 OCT.	**1988** AUG.	**1989** APRIL
Black Monday. The stock market crashes. The Dow-Jones Industrial Average loses 508 points, or 22.62%, erasing more than $500 billion from the value of U.S. stocks. The Toronto Stock Exchange 300 plunges 407.20 points, or 11.3%, wiping out $37 billion from the value of Canadian stocks.	Royal assent is given to Ottawa's plan to sell 45% of Air Canada, the sixteenth Crown corporation to be privatized since the Tories came to power in 1984. The remainder is sold the following year.	The federal government announces that a 9% national goods and services tax will be introduced in January 1991. The tax replaces the manufacturers' sales tax, which experts have called inefficient. In December, in response to protests, the GST rate is lowered to 7%.

The public's assessment of economic omens at the end of the 1980s was increasingly bleak. After seven years of growth, a recession of some kind seemed inevitable; in fact 53% predicted the economy would be worse in the next four to five years – the most pessimistic level of the entire decade. These convictions were all the more troubling because there was no longer one single, readily identifiable enemy, such as inflation or unemployment; and because our economic problems were perceived to be hostage to global factors – trade, currency differentials, flows of capital – over which even the national government had no real control. It was a recipe guaranteed to produce anxiety.

INTO THE NINETIES

In the 1980s, Canadians learned the lesson of economic uncertainty. In the 1990s, we will apply it. The central objective – in economics as in other areas – will be control. Patterns of investment will be characterized by the quest for security, an attempt to reduce uncertainty in an increasingly uncertain universe. Consumers will respond to fluctuations in interest rates, inflation, and other macroeconomic barometers more rapidly than we did in the 1980s. When next year's salary is not automatically higher than this year's salary, and progress is no longer a given, changes must be made. And Canadians know how to make them.

Retailers will find dealing with the 1990s consumer like dealing with a split personality. Where there is no apparent difference in value, the consumer will search for the best price. Where value is obvious, price will not matter. As a result, niche markets – specialty stores and boutiques – will continue to flourish, to the detriment of large, one-stop shopping palaces. Marketers will also have to provide more choice. Ever more cynical about products that claim to be new and improved, we will demand options that allow us to make up our own minds. In this multiple-choice society, all mass-market manufacturers will have to emulate Baskin-Robbins, offering a minimum of 31 flavours just to play the game.

In the past, retailers gained market share by offering the lowest prices and the greatest number of locations. But in the 1990s, changing patterns of consumption will make cutting profit

FACTS

Total foreign direct investment in Canada in 1983: $73.2 billion
Amount invested by Americans: $55.5 billion
Total foreign direct investment in 1987: $103.1 billion
Amount invested by Americans: $75.2 billion
Amount invested in Canada, through portfolios and directly, in 1970: $41.2 billion
Amount invested in 1980: $131.4 billion
Amount invested in 1987: $282 billion

Amount of net Canadian investment abroad in 1980: $2.7 billion
Amount invested abroad in 1989: $4.5 billion
Net foreign investment in Canada in 1980: $535 million
Net foreign investment in 1989: $3.4 billion

margins and spending capital on expansion a formula for bank-ruptcy. The message of the more effective mass merchandiser – Dave Nichols of Loblaws being the contemporary archetype – will be that its products are unique and available only at a few locations. Consumers will increasingly make up their minds about products after entering the store – so-called impulse buying. But an impulse buy is not an irrational buy. On the contrary, it says that purchasing decisions are being made not on the basis of advertising but on an examination of the product itself.

The pursuit of money is apt to be marked by some ambivalence in the 1990s. On the one hand, Canadians clearly want to slow down; on the other, they don't seem to know how. We want to spend more time with our families, yet we are working harder than ever. This gap between aspiration and experience will be filled in part by the growth of what might be called the actualization industry, companies and businesses that teach us – through gardening or yoga or flower arrangement – how to gain control over our lives.

We will expect help from government. In the past, governments created airlines, broadcasting systems, oil companies. Experience has now persuaded Canadians that running businesses is a task better left to the private sector. Not that leaving everything to private enterprise is a perfect answer. The last years of the 1980s taught us that the absence of government intervention in the economy can lead to an inequitable distribution of problems. So government will be as intrusive in the 1990s as it has been in the past, but it will be a different form of intrusion.

We will want politicians to set the rules – and to prosecute those who violate them. The rules might force developers to create more parkland and build schools as the price of a building permit. They might require pension plans, daycare centres, and parental-leave programs as the price of opening a business. They might demand that polluters allocate a specific percentage of gross profits to research and the development of environmental technology. Government will be more active in regulating product safety, the environment, packaging and labelling, all of the problems associated with involuntary risk. Government will be expected, in short, to bridge the chasm between private interest and public good. Corporations perceived to be pursuing their private interest at the expense of the public good will be called to account. The private sector is often slow to recognize that public opinion has an impact on its bottom line. For government, public opinion is the bottom line – and it will respond accordingly.

Canadians will continue to support the privatization of government agencies, believing that governments are inherently slothful and that government ownership is therefore inherently inefficient. This view is entirely pragmatic, not ideological. The operative test is: does it work? If privatization increases the efficiency of services delivered, the population will welcome it. If, on the other hand, it is seen to reduce services or efficiency, people will oppose it. (The same pragmatism will apply to free trade. As we enter the 1990s, most Canadians see more risk than reward in the free-trade agreement, which explains in part the lingering uncertainty about the future of the economy. But support for free trade will doubtless depend on whether the 1990s prove to be a decade of growth, prosperity and opportunity.)

The pressure to cut the federal deficit will build in the years ahead, and we will expect government to adapt as we have adapted – to be more prudent about spending and quicker to respond to changing economic conditions. Ottawa will probably be forced to sell assets – land and buildings. The other options – raising taxes and cutting spending – were exhausted in the 1980s and are increasingly less viable. If government were to resort to higher taxes, the prospect of a full-throttle tax revolt is remote. The Goods and Services Tax, although extremely unpopular, has not mobilized large portions of the population. Canada lacks a tradition of populist initiatives or referenda; most Canadians continue to regard the ballot box as the most effective form of political protest.

Overall, the 1990s are likely to be a decade of economic anxiety. Rapid change has become a constant, and our traditional cures no longer apply. Indeed, for the most part, Canadians find themselves sailing through uncertain waters without any sort of reliable behavioural compass. In the 1980s, most of us believed that we had failed to reach our full potential because conditions – inflation, recession, deficits – were aberrant. In the 1990s, we understand only too well that those developments were not aberrant – or, if they were, that aberrance has become the norm.

FACTS

Amount Canadians held in RRSPs in 1980: $3.676 billion Amount they held in 1987: $9.024 billion

Number of Canadians who invested in the stock market in 1983: 3.8 million Number in 1989: 4.3 million

Amount of mutual funds held by members of the Investment Funds Institute in 1980: $3.6 billion Amount in 1989: $23.5 billion Number of "balanced" mutual funds, considered more secure, offered by investment firms in 1987: 24 Number in December 1989: 68

FAMILY TIES

CHAPTER 7

"The root of the state is in the family."

MENCIUS

"There is nothing like staying at home for real comfort."

JANE AUSTEN

"Can we today measure devotion to husband and children by our indifference to everything else?"

GOLDA MEIR

THE 1980S ALTERED ATTITUDES TO EVERY MAJOR SOCIAL AND political institution in Canada. In the case of the Canadian family, they affected the very definition. The typical family once consisted of two parents (of opposite sexes), one or more of their children and, on occasion, a grandparent. That model was still in existence in the 1980s, but it was clearly an endangered species. Increasingly, the "family" was whatever living arrangement two or more people happened to arrive at. The varieties seemed to test the limits of statistical permutation: married men and women without children; single mothers or fathers with children; shared-custody situations; divorced men and women with new spouses (some without children, some with – from one or both previous marriages); common-law unions (with and without children); homosexual and bisexual relationships (sometimes with children); and all manner of communal societies.

The transformation of the basic family unit was accompanied

A MATTER OF DEGREES   The growing presence of women in the workplace
was driven primarily by education. In traditionally male fields, such
as law and medicine, the graduating classes were almost half female.

"I'm turning the dial down, not turning off the switch."

DAVE SANDERSON, A TORONTO MAR-
KETING DIRECTOR, ON HIS DECISION
TO SPEND MORE TIME WITH HIS
FAMILY, AFTER ARRIVING HOME FROM
A THREE-WEEK ROAD TRIP TO FIND
THAT HIS 18-MONTH-OLD SON DID NOT
RECOGNIZE HIM

by its shrinkage. More women were working outside the home; fewer were having babies. Those that did give birth tended to do so later in life, and they frequently returned to their outside jobs after maternity leave, enrolling their infants in daycare centres or leaving them at home with nannies. Women who wanted both career and an old-fashioned family life confronted a dilemma that was not easily resolved. Many men, too, had to reconcile their desire for more family time with their own professional ambitions – and with the fact that the "family" was often not around to spend time with. At a time when Canadians were expressing the desire to return to more traditional values, the traditions themselves were proving increasingly difficult to honour.

It was the inexorable rise of the working woman that did most to shape and define the Canadian family in the 1980s – and not without strain. In one 1983 survey, 65% of respondents said it would be better for children if mothers stayed home instead of going out to work; working women, predictably, were among those least likely to agree. And 48% contended that women would have to revert to their traditional role as homemakers if Canada were to overcome the problems it faced. Yet one year later, 76% acknowledged that, whatever their wishes might have been, attitudes towards female roles had changed.

Demographic forces seemed likely to keep them changing. Those who believed that working women were not less capable than working men, that married men should not be given preference for jobs over married women, and that women should not stay home with children tended to be younger and better educated, professional and often single – precisely those groups that would effect the greatest changes in the years ahead.

The growth of the female labour force was the result of several factors: higher levels of education, economic necessity, the decline of religions that preached "a woman's place is in the home" and, of course, the birth-control pill. But whatever the causes, the emergence of women in the workplace – in numbers that by the end of the decade were nearing parity with men – put a series of major policy issues on the national agenda: abortion, daycare, maternity (and paternity) leave, pay equity, affirmative action, flexible working hours, as well as divorce and custody questions in family law.

How Important is Your Job?

Is your career or job becoming a more
or less important part of your life?

December 1989

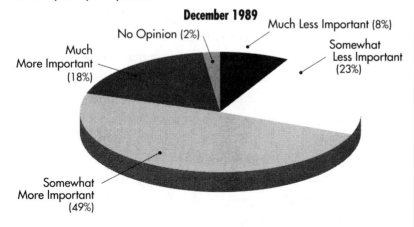

No Opinion (2%)

Much Less Important (8%)

Somewhat
Less Important
(23%)

Much
More Important
(18%)

Somewhat
More Important
(49%)

Why is Your Job Less Important?

December 1989

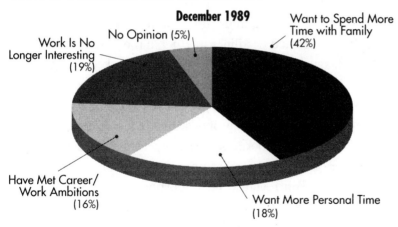

No Opinion (5%)

Work Is No
Longer Interesting
(19%)

Have Met Career/
Work Ambitions
(16%)

Want to Spend More
Time with Family
(42%)

Want More Personal Time
(18%)

Is Family Becoming More Important?

December 1989

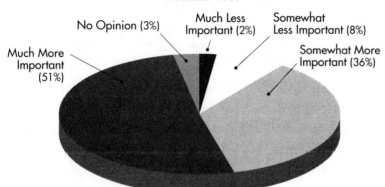

No Opinion (3%)

Much Less
Important (2%)

Somewhat
Less Important (8%)

Much More
Important
(51%)

Somewhat More
Important (36%)

Facts

**Fertility rate in
1986: 1.67 per
1,000 population
Rate in Northwest
Territories: 3.09
Rate in Quebec: 1.43**

**Number of Canadian
families in 1986:
6,734,980
Number in 1981:
6,667,631
Number of single-
parent families in
1986: 853,645
Number in 1981:
714,725**

**Rate of growth of
Canadian families in
the 1970s: 3.5%
In the 1980s: 2.2%
Projected growth
rate by the year
2000: 1%**

**Number of children
raised by single-
parent families in
1961: 500,000
Number in 1986:
1.2 million**

**Average number
of people in families
in 1977: 3.7
In 1981: 3.3
In 1986: 3.1**

"In addition, and in my view most important of all, she stayed home and looked after the children, his children."

MR. JUSTICE ALLEN AUSTIN, IN DECIDING TO AWARD A WOMAN WHO SEPARATED FROM HER COMMON-LAW SPOUSE AFTER 13 YEARS TOGETHER 40% OF THE VALUE OF THE HOUSE THEY SHARED

No issue was more fiercely fought than the abortion debate, especially after the 1988 Supreme Court ruling that declared the country's 1969 abortion law constitutionally invalid. Yet despite the level of rhetoric, Canadians displayed a remarkable degree of consensus on the matter. A solid majority – 60% in the spring of 1988 and 57% in the fall of 1989 – believed that in certain circumstances abortions should be permitted. Only about one in three respondents supported the pro-choice, abortion-on-demand argument; and only one in ten took the other extreme – the pro-life, "in no circumstances" position. Indeed, even among those who described themselves as pro-life, nearly 70% agreed that abortions should be permitted in certain circumstances. As for timing, 44% said abortions should be performed in the first 12 weeks of pregnancy or whenever a doctor feels it is necessary (44%); only 10% were willing to extend the period to 24 weeks.

Most respondents also endorsed high-court rulings that overturned abortion-barring injunctions granted by lower courts – an issue that dominated headlines in 1989 in the Barbara Dodd and Chantal Daigle cases. (Their boyfriends had asked the courts to prevent the women from having abortions.) In such disputes, 60% said the mother's rights should prevail; 33% said fetal rights were primary. Canadians generally oppose the right of anyone to use the courts to prevent an abortion; the decision should be left either to the mother or to the medical community. It was the latter opinion that Ottawa's controversial new abortion law was designed to reflect. Introduced in November 1989, it made abortion a criminal offence, unless a licensed doctor authorized the procedure on grounds of physical or emotional damage to the mother.

Working women who chose to bear children in the 1980s were legally entitled to 17 weeks' unpaid leave from their employers and 15 weeks of unemployment-insurance benefits. Most Canadians thought these benefits were fair; in fact, in a December 1986 survey 17% said they were too generous. A majority favoured enhancing UI – having Ottawa pay a third of a woman's salary during maternity leave – unless such a policy led to higher prices for consumers (in which case support fell to 37%). Overwhelmingly, Canadians felt that complications developed during pregnancy should be regarded as a short-term disability like any other, entitling women to collect disability benefits.

WOMEN IN THE WORK PLACE

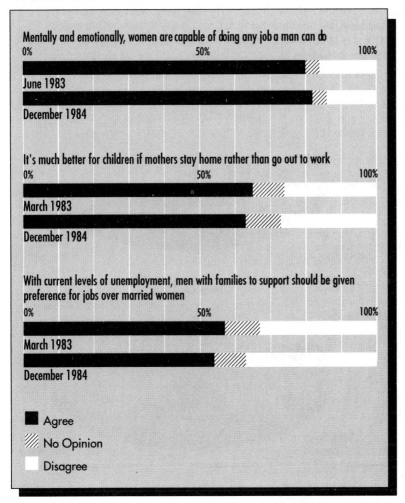

Mentally and emotionally, women are capable of doing any job a man can do

0%   50%   100%

June 1983

December 1984

It's much better for children if mothers stay home rather than go out to work

0%   50%   100%

March 1983

December 1984

With current levels of unemployment, men with families to support should be given preference for jobs over married women

0%   50%   100%

March 1983

December 1984

■ Agree

▨ No Opinion

☐ Disagree

FACTS

Percentage increase in number of childless families between 1981 and 1986: 9.3

Percentage increase in common-law relationships: 38.3

Percentage increase in married couples: 2.7

Percentage of all unions that were common-law in 1986: 8.3 – or 1 in 12 relationships

Percentage of all unions that were common-law relationships among men and women aged 20-24: 38 and 30 respectively

Percentage of common-law couples with children at home in 1981: 34.2

Percentage in 1986: 37.8

Percentage of married couples with children at home in 1981: 66.2

Percentage in 1986: 64.8

1980 DEC.

The Supreme Court of Canada, in a landmark decision, awards Rosa Becker half the assets accumulated during her 19-year common-law marriage – about $150,000. But legal delays and impediments prevent Becker from receiving any portion of the money, and in November 1986 she commits suicide.

1982 MAR.

Bertha Wilson becomes the first woman named to sit on the Supreme Court of Canada.

1983 JUNE

Dr. Henry Morgentaler opens an abortion clinic in Toronto.

"The court said a father has no rights, so why should a complete stranger have rights?"

ENSURING PAY EQUITY

The value of different jobs can be compared by rating skills required, effort expended, responsibilities, and working conditions. As a result, people with different jobs would be paid the same because their jobs would be considered of equal value to the employer. Would you support or oppose this kind of system to determine the value and pay range of jobs?

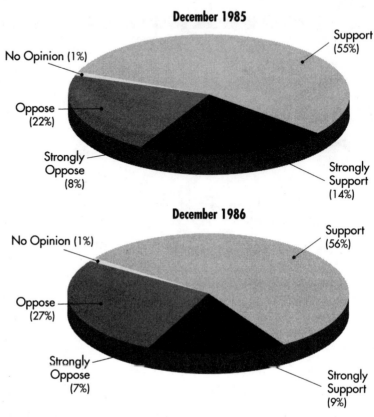

December 1985

No Opinion (1%)
Support (55%)
Oppose (22%)
Strongly Oppose (8%)
Strongly Support (14%)

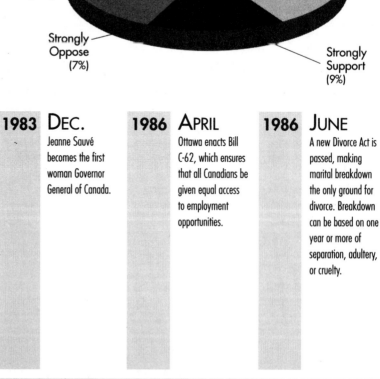

December 1986

No Opinion (1%)
Support (56%)
Oppose (27%)
Strongly Oppose (7%)
Strongly Support (9%)

1983 DEC.
Jeanne Sauvé becomes the first woman Governor General of Canada.

1986 APRIL
Ottawa enacts Bill C-62, which ensures that all Canadians be given equal access to employment opportunities.

1986 JUNE
A new Divorce Act is passed, making marital breakdown the only ground for divorce. Breakdown can be based on one year or more of separation, adultery, or cruelty.

CHILD CARE FOR EVERYONE?

Day-care services should be made available
to anyone who wants them

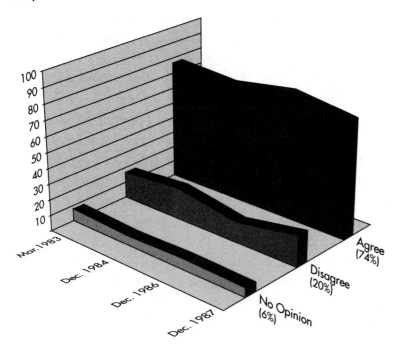

FACTS

**Percentage of families headed by divorced people in 1951: 3
Percentage in 1986: 30**

**Percentage of un-married women with children in 1961: 3
Percentage in 1986: 13**

**Percentage of women aged 30-34 who were single in Canada in 1986: 13.3
Percentage in Newfoundland: 9.6
Percentage in Quebec: 16.3**

**Number of single-parent families in 1986: 853,645
Percentage that were led by women: 82**

**Percentage of women in their thirties giving birth for the first time in 1970: 12
Percentage in 1986: 26**

1988 JAN.

The Supreme Court of Canada rules the federal law on abortion unconstitutional on the ground that it violates a woman's security of person. The decision leaves the nation in abortion limbo. The law had been in effect since 1969.

1988 JULY

The federal minister of health, Jake Epp, introduces the $6.4 billion Child Care Act, designed to improve daycare facilities across the country. The bill dies on the order paper in October, when a federal election is called. It is not reintroduced in the Conservative government's new term.

1988 NOV.

The province of Ontario passes legislation requiring employers with more than ten workers to pay women the same salaries as men for work of equal value. Similar legislation was already in place federally and in Manitoba and Quebec. It is now under consideration in other provinces.

"For a spouse without property, usually the wife, it's like finding her name on a lottery ticket. For the man, it's like getting shock therapy."

JIM STOFFMAN, A WINNIPEG LAWYER, ON THE IMPACT OF CHANGES IN THE COUNTRY'S DIVORCE LAWS, GRANTING EACH SPOUSE 50% OF ALL PROPERTY ACCUMULATED DURING THE LIFE OF THE MARRIAGE

The demand for improved daycare services, of course, was another natural consequence of rising levels of female employment. Three-quarters of Decima respondents agreed that child care should be available to anybody who wanted it; support was strongest among the young, the single, and working women. The problem with current daycare services, according to the survey, was either availability (37%) – there simply weren't enough spaces – or cost (36%). A smaller number (24%) thought the central issue was quality. But while Canadians clearly recognized the need for more and better daycare, a majority believed that the costs should be borne chiefly by parents, not government (29%) or employers (12%). On the other hand, people think government should play a role in providing quality, affordable daycare facilities, offering economic assistance either to parents, to employers, or directly to daycare centres themselves. And in 1987, six in ten said all daycare centres – profit-making or not – should be eligible for financial aid.

Within the workplace, there is solid support for the principle of pay equity – ensuring that men and women who perform work of equal value are paid the same salary; assessments of "equal value" are generally made on the basis of skills, effort, responsibility and working conditions. Three-quarters of Canadians say their employers are committed to treating men and women equally and are doing a good job at it. However, eight in ten respondents in a December 1986 survey said it would be difficult to create a fair system of evaluation. They were also concerned that such systems would raise costs and cause jobs to be lost. In fact, 38% said pay-equity schemes would lead to lower salaries for some employees. In part, these residual doubts may have been caused by the lack of credibility Canadians attached to the strongest advocates of pay equity – women's groups. Only 31% said they were more likely to believe information provided by women's organizations than information that came from private industry (27%), unions (21%), or government (18%). That statistic is particularly notable in that, on environmental and product-safety issues, seven in ten think environmental and consumer groups are the most credible sources of information.

More generally, large majorities of both men and women say the family, in whatever form, is becoming a more important part of their lives. The numbers are especially high among the so-called yuppie or baby-boom generation, and married men between

DIVORCE

Number of divorces in Canada in 1969: 26,000

Number in 1986: 78,160

Number in 1987: 86,985

Divorce rate among men aged 40-44 in 1971: 7.1 per 1,000 population

Rate in 1986: 15.7 per 1,000 population

Divorce rate among women aged 40-44 in 1971: 6.6 per 1,000 population

Rate in 1986: 14.2 per 1,000 population

Percentage decline in divorce rate between 1982-85: 14

Percentage increase in rate in 1986 after passage of new Divorce Act: 25

Provinces with highest divorce rate in 1986: Alberta (1,646 per 100,000 population) and B.C. (1,514 per 100,000 population)

Province with lowest rate: Newfoundland (469 per 100,000 population)

Percentage of women in divorce winning custody of children in 1986: 75

Percentage of men: 12

Percentage winning joint custody: 11

Percentage of cases awarding custody to third parties: 2

Percentage of fully paid-up support orders for divorced spouses in Ontario in 1989: 26

Percentage in Quebec: 50

MATERNITY BENEFITS

Number of women who collected maternity benefits in 1980: 107,336

Estimated number in 1989: 153,350

Year that Imperial Oil Ltd. first instituted a paternity-leave program, offering six months without pay but with full benefits: 1985

Number of employees who have applied since then: 12

FACTS

Percentage of married women working in 1971 with at least one child under age 6: 27
Percentage in 1986: 58

Percentage of all marriages in 1970 in which one spouse had been married before: 15.9
In 1980: 26.5
In 1987: 33

Percentage of women aged 65 and over living alone in 1961:15
Percentage in 1986: 34

Number of abortions reported as performed in 1970: 11,152
In 1980: 62,247
In 1986: 63,462
Estimated number of unreported abortions in the 1980s: 300,000

the ages of thirty and forty-four. In fact, asked in December 1988 to rate the relative priority attached to family, religion, and career, 77% chose family, 13% chose career; and 8% chose religion. At the same time, 40% agree that one can live a happy, rewarding life without children and 39% think the idea of marriage as we know it may be obsolete in ten or fifteen years. Those Canadians for whom family life is a growing priority do not regard it as incompatible with their professional ambitions. We are working harder, we enjoy our work (68% say they enjoy it a great deal), and we are proud of our achievements. Nevertheless, in December 1989, 31% of respondents reported that their jobs had become a less important part of their lives. And of that group, most cited the desire to spend more time with their families. Linked to other quality-of-life issues, it is a desire that seems likely to grow in the decade ahead.

INTO THE NINETIES

The desire to spend more time with family, a common motif in the late 1980s, is unlikely to wane in the years ahead. Turning it into a reality, however, will be a challenge, because several developments conspire against it.

One is the undeniable appeal of work, be it an eighty hour a week law practice in downtown Vancouver or a laser-welding assembly-line job in Brampton, Ont. The urge to succeed demands time and attention that are taken inevitably from the family. Another factor is the success of women in the workforce. Even a brief analysis of university enrolment in the professional disciplines signals the continuing breakdown of family life. In 1990, there were more women than men enrolled in Canadian colleges and universities. Women are nearing parity with men in law, medicine, and dentistry. In the 1990s they will achieve parity in the business schools. And exponential growth will occur in the classic male ghettos of mathematics, science, and engineering. By the end of the decade, women will draw even with men in the workplace.

But other societal trends also threaten the traditional family. The institution of marriage itself, once the prerequisite of "family," will continue to decline. Rising divorce rates, the dramatic growth of common-law relationships, the proliferation of

SUICIDE

The province of Quebec has the highest rate of teenage suicide in the world.

Estimated number of suicide attempts among adolescents in Quebec annually: 4,000

Suicide rate among teenagers in Canada in 1960: 3.3 per 100,000 population

The rate in 1986: 12.5

Number of suicides reported in Canada in 1986: 3,700 – or 14.6 per 100,000 population

Number reported between the early 1920s and early 1960s: 7.5 per 100,000 population

Percentage of Canadian deaths attributable to suicide since the late 1970s: 2

Percentage of suicides in 1986 that were male: just under 80

Suicide rate for men only in Canada in 1986: 22.8 per 100,000 population

Rate for Native Indian men: 56.3

Rate for Native Indian men aged 15-29: 100

FACTS

Number of first marriages per 1,000 population in 1971: 88
Number per 1,000 population in 1986: 57

First-marriage rate per 1,000 popula-tion among women aged 20-24 in 1971: 220
Number per 1,000 population in 1986: 107

Average age of women marrying in 1975: 24.75
Average age in 1980: 25.80
Average age in 1986: 27.75

Percentage of brides aged 25 and over in 1968: 22
Percentage in 1986: 50

1989 MARCH

The Supreme Court of Canada declines to issue a judgement on an appeal by Mani-toba's anti-abortion crusader Joe Borowski to have a fetus considered a human being pro-tected under the Charter of Rights.

1989 APRIL

The Canadian Human Rights Commission rules that homosex-ual couples can be considered families. The Commission was ruling on a case of a man denied bereave-ment leave to attend the funeral of a male partner's father by the federal Treasury Board and his union. The ruling was over-turned on appeal.

1989 AUG.

In a unanimous deci-sion, the Supreme Court of Canada strikes down a Quebec Court of Appeal ruling that granted Jean-Guy Trem-blay an injunction pre-venting his girlfriend, Chantal Daigle, from obtaining an abortion. One week before the Supreme Court rend-ers its decision, Daigle has an abortion in the United States.

"I think the fetus should have a right to life."

BARBARA DODD, ONE WEEK AFTER AN ABORTION AT DR. HENRY MORGEN-TALER'S TORONTO CLINIC. SHE HAD FOUGHT AN INJUNCTION AN ONTARIO COURT HAD GRANTED TO HER BOYFRIEND, WHICH WOULD HAVE BARRED THE PROCEDURE

QUALITY TIME   The baby boomers were less inclined to put their jobs ahead of their families as they discovered throughout the 1980s that the quality of their lives was as important as material success.

1989 SEPT.

The Canadian Advisory Council on the Status of Women receives a report saying four out of five sex-discrimination cases (35 out of 44) heard under the Charter of Rights and Freedoms were launched by men against laws designed to protect women from rape, or against maternity benefits and social assistance to single mothers.

1989 NOV.

The federal government introduces a bill that would make performing an abortion a criminal offence, but would allow abortions to be performed at any point in pregnancy upon the advice of a doctor if a woman's mental or physical health were threatened.

families that include the children of men and women married (or living common law) two or three times – these are formidable forces working against the explicit wish to improve the quality of life by spending more time with family.

For the moment, the conflict between that wish and the forces inhibiting its realization is not widely recognized. As the baby boomers grow older, however, the contradiction will become at once more apparent and more aggravating, accelerating the demand for solutions. In the 1990s, companies will offer employment to both husband and wife and provide daycare for their children. The environment may be non-traditional, but families will spend more time together – during lunches, coffee breaks, etc. – than they would otherwise. Employers that do not create a pool of basic benefits – from pension plans to pay equity, from parental leaves to on-site daycare – will face severe competitive pressure from those that do. These benefits will be designed primarily to entice, retain, and reward women, who (apart from immigrants) will constitute the only growth segment in employment. There will be no growth in male employment in the 1990s.

If business fails to respond to the needs of the family, people will demand that government use its legislative leverage to force accommodations. Technology will help, enabling men and women to work at home, linked to their offices by computer, fax machine, and modem. In the interest of family life, some couples will work at home all the time, serving multiple employers on a contract basis. This may have an impact on the birth rate, which has been in decline for three decades, a reverse image of the trend line that charts women in the workforce. Indeed, if more Canadians work at home or bring their children to work, the 1990s might produce the first real echo to the baby boom of the late 1940s and 1950s.

The aging of the boom generation will also force us to change our definitions of "old." Many experts have assumed that the next generation of senior citizens will behave the way previous generations did; and that the rest of the population will react to them in exactly the same way. But the next generation of elderly Canadians is certain to be the most active and healthy the country has ever known. Compulsory retirement will be abolished, because the elderly will constitute a resource of talent, experience, and wisdom that cannot be replaced.

FACTS

Percentage of never-married women aged 25-29 in 1961: 15
Percentage in 1986: 26

Number of solved cases of homicides in Canada from 1974-87: 7,582
Percentage that involved a family member: 39

Number of licensed or provincially approved daycare spaces in Canada in 1980: 109,141
Number in 1988: 263,659

Percentage of women in the workforce in 1970: 38.3
Percentage in 1980: 50.3
Percentage in 1988: 57.4

ACCESS TO ABORTION
Women should be allowed to have abortions...

March 1988

Under No Circumstances (10%)

No Opinion (1%)

On Demand (29%)

Under Certain Circumstances (60%)

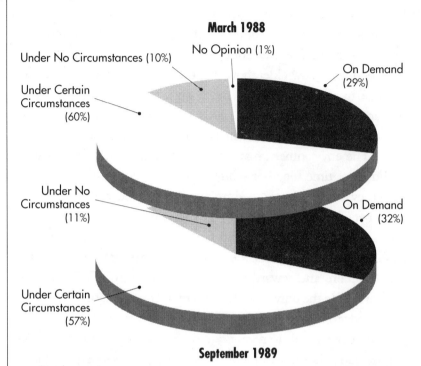

Under No Circumstances (11%)

On Demand (32%)

Under Certain Circumstances (57%)

September 1989

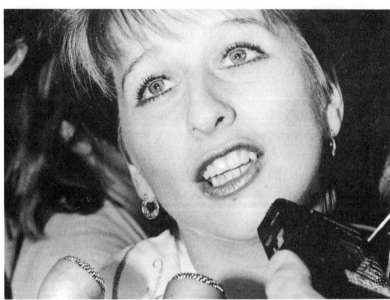

THE GREAT DEBATE   Chantal Daigle, the Quebec woman who sought an abortion against the wishes of her boyfriend, symbolized the country's deep and apparently irreconcilable division on the issue of abortion.

On the other hand, the elderly may be a less integral part of the family in the 1990s. One reason is money. Poverty in Canada is no longer a function of age. The percentage of Canadians over the age of sixty-five who live below the poverty line has dropped in the past twenty years from 50 to less than 15. Rising real-estate values and the cumulative growth of registered retirement savings plans have given the elderly a previously unknown level of economic security. Healthier than ever before, and more afflu-ent, old people will be less dependent on family. Instead of being handy babysitters or financial and emotional burdens, grandpar-ents will be just as likely to go cruising in the Caribbean or on safari in Africa.

What seems unlikely to change in the 1990s is the growth in single-parent families. But here, too, government may play a role. For decades, income has been transferred to single mothers with no appreciable impact on the quality of their lives. In the next decade, government may experiment with other solutions, offering free daycare to enable more women to work, or combining daycare with an education voucher to enable women with high-school cre-dentials to earn university degrees. (The universities would waive tuition.) Such reforms would reduce the high numbers of single parents now living below the poverty line. At the same time, they would make it much easier to become a single parent, giving women more discretionary income and more control over their lives.

These are not the images that leap to mind when Canadians think about family. But the transformation of family life that occurred in the 1980s seems certain to continue, posing new chal-lenges and requiring new adaptations.

FACTS

Number of women working in the service sector in 1981: 2.1 million
Number in that sector in 1986: 2.4 million
Average hourly wage of unionized female employees in the service sector in 1986: $12.53
Average hourly wage of non-unionized female employees: $9.17

Percentage of women among graduates in medicine in 1980: 32.3
Percentage in 1989: 44.2

Percentage of women among graduates in law in 1980: 15-20
Percentage in 1986: 36
Percentage in 1989: about 50

SEX AND OTHER RECREATIONS

CHAPTER 8

"Lord, make me chaste – but not yet."

ST. AUGUSTINE

THE DECISIVE EVENT OF THE 1980S – AT LEAST IN TERMS OF Canadian attitudes to sex – was the Acquired Immune Deficiency Syndrome (AIDS) epidemic. Medical detectives have not yet determined exactly when it began, but its impact on public opinion was immense, engendering a conservatism in sexual behaviour that was born out of fear.

Decima first registered misgivings in 1985, when a fifth of respondents said they were "very concerned" that they might personally contract the disease. This anxiety had little to do with sexual activity; indeed, people who said they had not had sex in twelve months indicated higher levels of concern about AIDS than people who had had four or more sexual partners. But in the first wave of publicity about the disease, few were inclined to change their sexual behaviour: 82% said AIDS had not changed their habits.

The likeliest to be affected were the sexually active, those reporting four or more partners in one year; 36% of these respondents said the epidemic had in fact affected their sexual behaviour. Women were 6% likelier than men to voice fears about AIDS, but less likely to say their habits had changed as a result. Of course, women generally reported less sexual contact than men – and may therefore have been less at risk. More sexually active, men were also more inclined to exercise caution, although heterosexuals

EPIDEMIC PROPORTIONS   Two mourners at a memorial in Montreal for victims
of AIDS. Incidence of the disease was highest among homosexuals, but it
encouraged more conservative sexual behaviour among all Canadians.

considered themselves unlikely to encounter the high-risk AIDS groups – homosexuals and drug addicts.

In 1986, fewer Canadians claimed to be "very or somewhat" sexually active, and more people acknowledged being not very or not at all engaged in sex. More dramatic changes occurred in 1987. Levels of monogamy rose 3%, the "very or somewhat" sexually active category dropped by a full 10% and the "not too active" figures climbed 13%. The impact of AIDS was unmistakable, especially on the young, on students, on singles, and on those with several sexual partners. A majority of respondents continued to insist that their sexual life styles had been unaffected; but in overwhelming numbers, Canadians were (or claimed to be) monogamous – and hence saw no need to change sexual behaviour.

Surveys in 1989 confirmed these trends. Some 53% of respondents said they were very or somewhat concerned about contracting AIDS (compared with 46% in 1985). And 26% reported that the spread of such diseases had changed their sexual habits to some extent (compared with 12% in 1985). Not surprisingly, the greater the concern about AIDS, the greater the likelihood of modified sexual behaviour. Still, a vast majority doubted they would ever be victims of the disease; 50% said their chances of contracting it were "absolutely zero."

Whatever their views about AIDS, most Canadians were not influenced by advertisements and appeals to use condoms. In 1989, only 7% said they regularly carried condoms. And only 13% said they routinely used them; in fact, 72% said they never – or rarely – did. Predictably, condom use was significantly higher among students (35%), single people (33%), those without children (30%), and those with multiple sexual partners (36%); only 10% of those who reported a single sex partner said they used condoms.

Most Canadians, of course, knew AIDS in the abstract; in 1989, only 12% reported knowing an AIDS victim. But our ignorance catalysed our fear. A third of respondents said they were concerned about AIDS in the workplace, and 65% said it was either very or somewhat important to establish an AIDS policy at work – to protect those without the disease, not victims.

In the public's mind, AIDS was associated largely with homosexuals, a sexual preference for which most Canadians seem to have a fair degree of tolerance. Although only 24% described their feelings toward homosexuals as sympathetic, another 56% said they were neutral. And while almost a fifth claimed that AIDS had made them more hostile toward homosexuals, 69% said the epidemic had not changed their basic views. (By a margin of 12 percentage points, women were likelier than men to be tolerant of homosexuality.)

In 1988, Decima asked Canadians what they would do if they learned that their doctor or dentist, an employee, a senior politician of their party, or their child's teacher was homosexual. Again, respondents were generally accepting. Indeed, in the case of the politician and the employee, more than three-quarters said they would do nothing about it. There was less equanimity, however, about the other professionals: 35% said they would either try to have a child with a homosexual teacher moved to another class or seek to have the teacher removed from the school system; and 39% said they would change doctors or dentists.

The 1980s were characterized by freedom of sexual expression. Yet most Canadians remained reticent about declaring their own sexual orientations. In one 1985 survey, only 1% described themselves as bisexual and only .25% identified themselves as homosexual. Nor did these figures change radically in later years. Despite that reserve, more than three-quarters believed in 1984 that attitudes toward sex had become more permissive in the past twenty years, although a majority said the change had not been beneficial to Canadian society in general. By 1989, however, the AIDS factor had changed the perception of promiscuity: 39% said the trend line was either flat or in decline.

Overall, most people pronounced themselves satisfied with their sexual lives. The numbers were particularly high for employed women and those living common law; they were particularly low for single and divorced respondents, and those 18-19 years of age. The weekend is clearly Canadians' preferred time for sex; 87% said in 1986 that the sexual act is performed either Friday (20%), Saturday (51%) or Sunday (16%). Week nights rated no better than 5%.

Among those who were married, about 12% admitted to having an adulterous relationship, although only 8% said they were aware that their spouses had had affairs. Among those most likely to commit adultery were people living common law (24%), Montrealers (19%), atheists and agnostics or non-observing disciples of

FACTS

The average work week in manufacturing
1960: 39.8 hours
In 1970: 39.1 hours
In 1980: 37.9 hours
In 1989: 38.6 hours

Estimated number of golfers in 1980:
1.1 million
Number in 1989:
2.2 million

Estimated amount of money generated by bird-watching in Canada in 1986:
$4 billion
Estimated number of jobs created: 86,000
Estimated tax revenues generated:
$900 million

Percentage of Canadian homes with colour television sets in 1975: 53.4
Percentage in 1980: 81.1
Percentage in 1989: 96

religion (19%), and those 45-49 years old. About two-thirds of those who had had affairs said the experience had left no physical or emotional scars. Women were twice as likely as men to say they had been harmed by such an experience. About 25% of the time, extra-marital affairs led to marriage breakdown. But in many cases, men and women responded to the knowledge of their spouses' infidelity by doing nothing.

Sexual behaviour aside, it is clear that more Canadians were devoting leisure time to the pursuit of health and fitness. In March 1988, four out of five respondents said they were somewhat or much more concerned about health and fitness than they had been five years earlier; and 75% said their concern had produced changes in life style. Typically, these involved diet and weight control, although large numbers also claimed to exercise regularly, manage stress, and have an annual physical check-up.

Through the decade, Decima asked several questions testing attitudes towards money and leisure time. The results generally confirm the classic Canadian stereotype of cautious savers. Between 1980 and 1986, a majority said they would rather save their money for retirement than spend it. (British Columbians were most likely to be spenders.) Two out of three maintained they would rather spend money on a house than on travel. (New Brunswickers were most likely to be in the minority.) And most people said they would rather eat dinner at home than in a restaurant – although the number had declined 9 percentage points by 1986.

On two occasions, respondents were also offered the ultimate in leisure-time scenarios: a choice of things to do if they were stranded on a desert island. The results were both consistent and surprising. Some 70% said they would prefer to spend time either with their current partner or spouse or with an attractive person of the opposite sex. Only 14% said they would want a library of all the books one would ever want to read; only 6% chose a television set with all the channels and videos available; and only 3% opted for all the music one might ever want to listen to. These choices suggest that for most Canadians leisure time is best spent not in solitary activities, but in the company of loved ones.

How's Your Sex Life?

Would you describe yourself as...

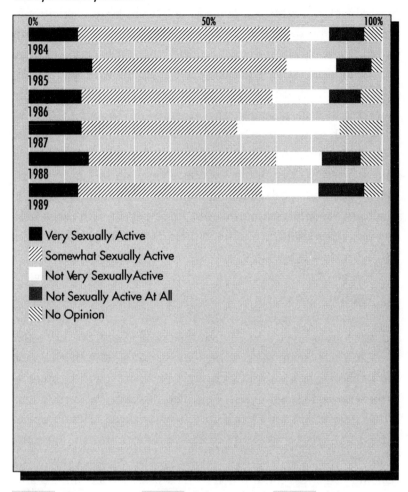

0%	50%	100%
1984		
1985		
1986		
1987		
1988		
1989		

■ Very Sexually Active
▨ Somewhat Sexually Active
□ Not Very Sexually Active
■ Not Sexually Active At All
▧ No Opinion

1981 Dec.

Trivial Pursuit, a board game invented by Christopher Haney and Scott Abbott of Montreal, is made available commercially. By the end of the decade, nine versions of the game had been created and were being distributed in 21 languages in 27 countries. Global sales had reached $41 million.

1982 March

Downhill skier Steve Podborski becomes the first Canadian to win the World Cup.

1982 May

Quebec-born Gilles Villeneuve, six-time winner of the Grand Prix auto race, dies while training for the Belgian Grand Prix.

"We must make
condoms as
freely available
to kids as
aspirin."

ART WOOD, A SPOKESMAN FOR THE AIDS
COMMITTEE OF TORONTO, URGING THE
BOARD OF EDUCATION TO INSTALL
CONDOM DISPENSERS IN THE CITY'S HIGH
SCHOOLS, SEPTEMBER 1989

INTO THE NINETIES

Several factors suggest exponential growth in leisure activities in the decade ahead. One is the importance of quality of life, which will dramatically change our approach to health, nutrition, fitness, and general life style. Increasingly, Canadians will seek to gain greater control of their lives. This phenomenon is reflected in the emerging self-actualization and personal-empowerment industries, which teach people how to cut back on 70-hour work weeks and other time-consuming commitments. In the 1990s, people will discover that leisure is not simply an end in itself, but a means to a greater end: wellbeing. And the aging of a healthier – and far wealthier – population means that more people with disposable incomes large enough to indulge their desires will be looking for new leisure challenges.

Some of this is already in evidence. In 1980, exotic travel – photographic safaris to Kenya, mountain climbing in Nepal, bicycle tours through the Italian Alps, boat excursions down the Amazon – was a rarity. In 1990, it is commonplace. So, too, is the four- and five-day mini-vacation – a long weekend in Bermuda or the Bahamas, or a week at some upscale resort spa that caters to the whole person, with classes on diet, exercise and meditation. Other choices will proliferate in the years ahead. Holidays that expose us to risk – two weeks in the Caribbean sun and the consequent threat of skin cancer – are losing their appeal. Conversely, holidays that stress communion with nature, such as camping and fishing, are becoming far more popular. So are sports that complement the rise of environmental consciousness – golf, hiking and bird-watching, for example – although the shift to less stressful forms of recreation is also related to the aging population. A decade of relentless jogging has taught us that other cardiovascular activities can do as much for the heart and lungs, with fewer injuries to joints and ligaments.

The determined quest for better health – a subliminal search for immortality – shows no sign of abating. As with the environment, an entire vocabulary of wellness is entering the language. Many Canadians can now recite the benefits of high-impact versus low-impact aerobics, the daily recommended intake of sodium chloride, and the foods that are said to contribute to the good,

THE QUEST FOR HEALTH (MARCH 1988)

Are you and your family...

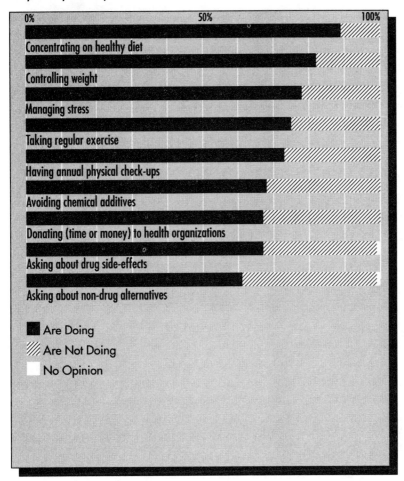

0%	50%	100%

Concentrating on healthy diet

Controlling weight

Managing stress

Taking regular exercise

Having annual physical check-ups

Avoiding chemical additives

Donating (time or money) to health organizations

Asking about drug side-effects

Asking about non-drug alternatives

■ Are Doing

/// Are Not Doing

☐ No Opinion

1982 OCT.

Pianist Glenn Gould, 50, dies of a stroke.

1982 NOV.

The Applebaum-Hébert report on cultural policy in Canada is issued. It urges more Canadian content in film and television and recommends greater funding for the arts generally.

1985 DEC.

Royal assent is given to Bill C-49, an anti-soliciting law that says that both prostitutes and their clients may be prosecuted if they communicate in public for the sale or purchase of sex. The law is challenged as a violation of freedom of expression under the Charter of Rights. In June 1990, a Supreme Court of Canada ruling upholds the law.

FACTS

Percentage of Canadian males who smoked daily in 1981: 36.7
Percentage in 1986: 30.8
Percentage of Canadian females who smoked in 1981: 28.9
Percentage in 1986: 25.8

Number of litres of beer per person per year consumed by Canadians in 1980: 113.55
Number in 1985: 105.65

Number of litres of wine per person per year consumed by Canadians in 1980: 11
Number in 1985: 12.4
Number of litres of spirits per person per year consumed by Canadians in 1980: 10.51
Number in 1985: 8.53

"There is a moral crisis in sport – not only in Canada, but on a world-wide scale."

ROBERT ARMSTRONG, CHIEF COUNSEL TO THE DUBIN INQUIRY, OCTOBER 1989

AIDS

Number of cases of AIDS reported in Canada in June 1990: 3,824

Number of AIDS-related fatalities: 2,282 (59.7%)

Percentage of cases affecting males: 93

Percentage of cases in high-risk categories (homosexuals and bisexuals): 84

Province with the highest concentration of AIDS cases: British Columbia (232.7 per 1 million population)

Estimated number of Canadians thought to have tested positive for AIDS: 30,000-50,000

Year first AIDS case was reported in Canada: 1982

Number of new cases of AIDS reported in the U.S. in 1988: 27,975

Number reported from 1981-1988: 87,545

Percentage of cases involving homosexuals, drug abusers, or both: 89

Percentage involving heterosexuals: 4

Percentage involving blood transfusions: 3

1986 MAY
Expo 86 opens in Vancouver. More than 22 million visitors attend before it closes in October.

1987 MAY
Justice Minister Ray Hnatyshyn tables a sweeping anti-pornography bill in the House of Commons. Bill C-54 stirs a storm of controversy and dies on the order paper; it is not reintroduced.

1988 FEB.
Calgary hosts the Winter Olympics, which ultimately earn a $46-million profit.

THE FITNESS FAD

Would you say that Canadians/
you are... about personal health and fitness
than in the recent past

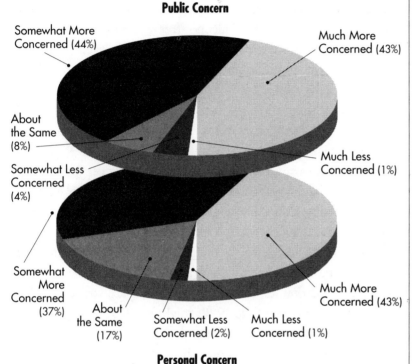

Public Concern

Somewhat More
Concerned (44%)

Much More
Concerned (43%)

About
the Same
(8%)

Somewhat Less
Concerned
(4%)

Much Less
Concerned (1%)

Somewhat
More
Concerned
(37%)

About
the Same
(17%)

Somewhat Less
Concerned (2%)

Much Less
Concerned (1%)

Much More
Concerned (43%)

Personal Concern

FACTS

Amount collected by
Ottawa in excise taxes
on alcohol and
tobacco in 1964-65:
$629 million
Amount in 1980-81:
$1.508 billion
Amount in 1988-89:
$2.705 billion

Amount of time on
average devoted to
television viewing in
1976: 3.2 hours
per day
Amount in 1987: 3.4
hours per day
Amount for women:
3.8 hours per day
Group that watches
the least: men, aged
18-24
Group that watches
the most: women,
aged 60 and over
Percentage of televi-
sion watching devoted
to drama: 33
Percentage of drama
that originated in
Canada: 4.2
Province that watched
the most television in
1987: Newfoundland
Province that watched
the least: Alberta

1988 AUG.

Wayne Gretzky,
Canada's premier
hockey player, is
traded by Edmonton
Oiler owner Peter
Pocklington to the
Los Angeles Kings.

1988 SEPT.

Sprinter Ben Johnson
wins the 100-metre
race at the Seoul
Summer Olympics in
a world-record 9.73
seconds but is re-
quired to forfeit his
gold medal days later
for taking banned
steroids. An earlier
world record is also
erased, and Johnson
is banned from com-
petition for two years.

1989 JAN.

An inquiry into the use
of drugs in sports
opens under Charles
Dubin, the chief justice
of Ontario. In June
1990, he recom-
mends that Johnson
and other Canadian
athletes who took
steroids should lose
federal financial
support, but that
sports federations
determine eligibility
for competition.

"We cannot treat as a crime that which the legislature has deliberately refrained from making a crime."

MADAM JUSTICE BERTHA WILSON, IN WRITING THE JUNE 1990 MINORITY OPINION OF THE SUPREME COURT OF CANADA ON THE CONSTITUTIONALITY OF THE FEDERAL GOVERNMENT'S 1985 ANTI-SOLICITING LAW

rather than the bad, kind of cholesterol. More will be able to do so in the 1990s, and their knowledge will influence their behaviour. But with wellness goes indulgence – or what Decima calls "occasionality." After two hours of weight-training in the gym, a few ounces of 20%-butterfat Haagen-Dazs ice-cream are a reward deserved. After a week of alcohol-free lunches and dinners, a snifter of premium cognac on the weekend may seem an entitlement. Still, such indulgences will be more discreet than in the past and more driven by events – celebrations of one sort or another.

Some leisure activities – drinking and driving for one, smoking for another – have clearly reached a point of no return. Both have become socially reprehensible and totally indefensible. What crippled smoking was not so much the link with cancer, but the evidence that even non-smokers, exposed to secondary smoke for long periods of time, were at significant risk. The same, of course, applies to the innocent victims of drunk drivers. This is an omen for the 1990s. The do-your-own-thing ethic that was popular in the 1960s will be qualified in the years ahead, especially where matters of health, nutrition, environment and fitness are concerned. The dominant philosophy of the 1990s might be "Do your own thing," but not if it encroaches on someone else's wellbeing. Indeed, people whose life styles are inconsistent with the norm may become targets of messianic appeals, exhorted not to salt their eggs, eat too much butter, buy products wrapped in non-biodegradable materials, etc. Searching for a better quality of life, many Canadians are likely to acquire something of the missionary spirit.

A major question is what will happen to more traditional forms of recreation – reading, music, watching TV with the family. All of those activities scored low in one recent Decima survey. The rise of interactive games – Nintendo, Sega, Atari – may further this trend. The younger generation of Canadians seems increasingly less enamoured of passive, solitary forms of recreation. The libraries of the nation are empty; the video parlours are crowded.

Despite impressive technological advances, the mass introduction of high-density television, digital audio tape, and fibre optics may be postponed well into the decade. The issue is cost versus value: HDTV may deliver a clearer image than conventional television, but the difference is not as radical as the one that marked the arrival of colour. The same is true for digital audio tape; again,

SPEND OR SAVE?

I would rather spend the money I make now than save it for retirement

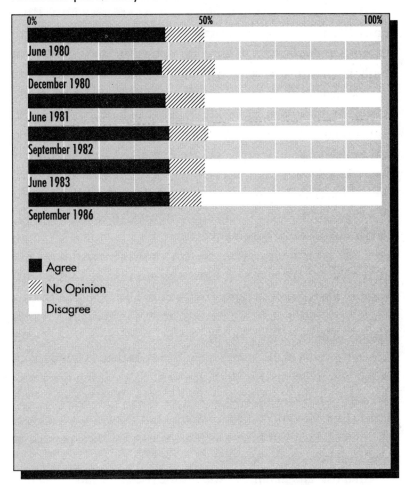

0%   50%   100%

June 1980

December 1980

June 1981

September 1982

June 1983

September 1986

■ Agree

▨ No Opinion

☐ Disagree

FACTS

What the federal government spent on recreation and culture in 1980-81: $539.1 million
What it spent in 1989-90: $1.4708 billion

Number of hours Canadians spent daily in leisure pursuits in the 1980s: 5.5
Number of Canadians claiming to participate in recreational activities in 1981: 20.7 million
Percentage that claimed walking as activity of choice: 57.2
Bicycling: 37.8
Swimming: 36.2
Jogging: 31.2
Gardening: 29.8
Curling: 4.8

Percentage of Canadians who claimed walking as an exercise in 1988: 63
Percentage that claimed gardening: 52
Percentage that claimed jogging: 18

1989 JUNE
The $500-million Skydome opens in Toronto, featuring a 7,000-ton retractable roof.

1989 JUNE
An Alberta Human Rights Board inquiry rules that a man who tested positive for AIDS was unjustly dismissed for failing to report his condition to his employer.

1989 SEPT.
Toronto homosexual James Saccary is barred entrance to the United States on the ground that he is a sexual deviant.

"We find our-selves in the anomalous – some would say bizarre – situation where almost every-thing relating to prostitution has been regulated by the criminal law except the transaction itself."

MR. JUSTICE ANTONIO LAMER, WRITING THE MAJORITY OPINION OF THE COURT UPHOLDING THE 1985 LAW

the product is superior, but the difference does not compare to the impact that more portable tapes and compact discs had on the record industry. Besides, as Sony learned to its regret with its Beta-format video tapes, technical superiority alone does not guarantee marketplace dominance. Cinephiles flocked to the VHS format simply because it delivered what they wanted most: more films.

No new technology will spawn a completely different leisure life style in the 1990s, and this may produce boredom with both form and content. Already, traditional television programming is on the decline. With few exceptions, Canadians don't regard any single television series as must viewing. On the other hand, special events – the Academy Awards, the Stanley Cup Playoffs, the first TV screening of a popular film – generate high ratings. The commercial response is to turn every concert, film, book and TV mini-series into a marketing event, so that consumers feel they can't afford to be left out. Cultural superstars will flourish in this environment; the rest will struggle. In pop music, for instance, the top ten artists will sell millions of records, while the also-rans flirt with oblivion. The top ten itself will be increasingly eclectic, with various "flavours of the month" (typified in the late 1980s by Milli Vanilli, New Kids on the Block, Paula Abdul) sharing the charts with such durable celebrities as Phil Collins, Rod Stewart, Tina Turner, Paul Simon, Paul McCartney, et al. New musical genres will enjoy sudden but brief success, the basis of their popularity being their very unpredictability.

In music and in film, we will see the rise of the independents, and the formation of new, symbiotic relationships between established multinational studios and young, more creative producers. The corporations will provide the seed capital, in exchange for first rights of refusal on the product. In Canada, these young producers will shift their focus – at least in terms of target markets – from the limited domestic audience of 26 million to the global market of consumers who want to hear or see or read the Canadian perspective. More generally, the 1990s will usher in a new era of realism in the arts. This is part of the larger search for universal truth and veracity, and the growing aversion to sham, deception and pretence.

In matters of sex, two trends are clear. First, we are set more firmly than ever before on a course toward monogamy. Second, abstinence among singles is more common than sex, safe or otherwise. What lies behind this behaviour is fear, the exposure to risk that cannot be measured because it cannot be seen. Sexual disease – particularly AIDS – is the consummate involuntary risk. In the absence of much wider distribution and use of condoms – only 6% of Canadians now carry them – these patterns are certain to continue. Singles bars, prostitution and other phenomena seen as promoting promiscuity will decline in the 1990s. Conversely, pornography and erotica, which offer fantasy without risk, may not.

AIDS and concern about homosexuality and pedophilia have put clear limits on the tolerance of Canadians to alternative sexual life styles. This, too, seems likely to continue. As people become more monastic, they will take an increasingly dim view of those who indulge in behaviour potentially harmful to innocents. Many Canadians regard homosexuality as aberrant, and AIDS has made them somewhat more hostile to the homosexual world generally. None of the trends bode well for any major attitudinal changes.

FACTS

Percentage of Canadians who claimed to exercise three hours per week in 1981: 56
Percentage in 1988: 75

Number of Ontario companies that, by 1989, had introduced fitness and/or wellness programs: 800

Amount Canadians spend on recreation annually: $5 billion
Percentage of Canadians who claim to engage in some form of recreation: 25

Rank of tourism among Canadian exports by industry in 1988: 3 (motor vehicles and auto parts were 1 and 2 respectively)
Estimated annual revenues from tourism in 1988: $24 billion
Estimated amount spent by Canadians: $17.3 billion

THE SWINGING GATE

CHAPTER 9

"Without immigration, continuation of Canada's below-replacement fertility rate would gradually lead to Canada's disappearance."
                                                    STATISTICS CANADA, 1989

"I think a stalwart peasant in a sheepskin coat, born on the soil, whose forefathers have been farmers for ten generations, with a stout wife and a half-dozen children, is good quality."
SIR CLIFFORD SIFTON, MINISTER OF THE INTERIOR, 1896-1905
                                          (The remark was made in 1922)

WHEN IT COMES TO IMMIGRATION, THERE ARE CLEARLY TWO Canadas. One is humane, philanthropic, understanding; the other is intolerant and latently racist. This is regrettable, perhaps, but true.

Canadians firmly endorse the principle of immigration; indeed, we regard our generosity to less-advantaged peoples of other races, religions, and cultures as one of our finer qualities. But the reality of immigration is apparently more troublesome. The ambivalence showed up in Decima surveys throughout the 1980s. In September 1987, 74% said that our tradition of welcoming people of diverse backgrounds was one of the best things about Canada. Only one in five disagreed with that proposition.

But our charity has limits. For most of the decade, a large majority of Canadians consistently opposed open – that is, unlimited – immigration. Between September 1981 and September 1987, Decima asked respondents whether "anyone who wants to

CULTURAL FUSION   The arrival of the first significant wave of non-white immigration dramatically altered the demographic composition of Canadian cities in the 1980s – and the process has only just begun.

"Go home trash."

A PLACARD OUTSIDE THE STADACONA NAVAL BASE IN HALIFAX, WHERE 174 ILLEGAL REFUGEES FROM INDIA WERE TEMPORARILY BEING HOUSED IN JULY 1987

Peanut butter and jelly sandwiches.

WHAT KATHLEEN GOREHAM SERVED THE EAST INDIANS A FEW DAYS EARLIER IN WOODS HARBOUR, N.S.

"Ms. McDougall is really missing the boat."

LIBERAL IMMIGRATION CRITIC SERGIO MARCHI, AFTER THE CONSERVATIVE IMMIGRATION MINISTER ANNOUNCED THAT CANADA WOULD ACCEPT 20,000 REFUGEES IN 1990, THE SAME NUMBER AS IN 1989

"Canada is a peculiar nation. Peopled by immigrants, it is a country that hates and fears immigration."

IRVING ABELLA, AUTHOR OF *NONE IS TOO MANY*, JANUARY 1988

should be able to immigrate to Canada." The number disagreeing with that statement was never less than 66%; the number agreeing was never more than 27%.

The pattern was consistent in every part of the country and in every age group. Westerners and Canadians of British descent were particularly hard-line. But so, ironically, were Canadians of non-British and non-French ancestry – the very ethnic groups that Canadian immigration policies over the decades had welcomed. Resident Canadians, no matter how recent their residence, regard immigrants as threats. The most receptive by far, according to a September 1987 poll, were French Canadians – 42% favouring open immigration. The least: British Columbians (12%), probably as a result of a recent wave of Asian immigrants.

In the summer of 1989, Decima put the same question in a slightly different way, asking whether Canadians would support immigration beyond the government's targeted 1988 level – 160,000. Only 12% said they would; 54% favoured reductions. (Significantly, the same groups that generally favour more immigration – wealthier, better educated, professionals – reject the notion that immigration policies represent one of the best aspects of Canadianness. What they're rejecting, of course, is not immigration but the policies themselves; in their view, they are not generous enough.)

We are more liberal on the issue of encouraging skilled tradesmen to come to Canada, but our views are clearly influenced by economic conditions. Before the country plunged into deep recession in 1981, 54% agreed that Ottawa should reach out to skilled workers abroad and help them to immigrate; only 36% disagreed. Three years later, with the worst of the recession over, but unemployment still high (11.2%), the percentages had reversed themselves. Fifty-four percent opposed immigration by skilled tradesmen; 36% still endorsed it.

The impact of the recession was critical. In the summer of 1982, Canadians regarded unemployment as the nation's most important problem. And levels of concern rose steadily for the next two years. Many perceived a real threat to their jobs – and hence to their overall wellbeing. In that context, it is hardly surprising that a majority wanted the federal government to deter yet another threat and close the gates to immigrants. (Ottawa complied.)

OPENING THE DOOR
Anyone who wants to immigrate to Canada should be allowed to do so

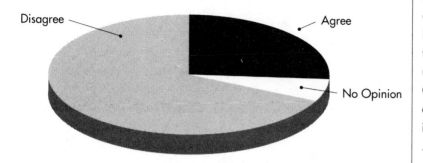

THE CASE FOR SKILLED IMMIGRANTS
Those who have a skilled trade should be encouraged to immigrate to Canada

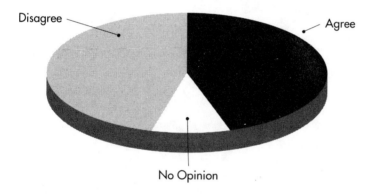

FACTS

In 1913, Canada accepted 400,000 immigrants – 5% of the nation's total population. In the 1980s, Canada accepted an average of 125,000 immigrants a year – .5% of the total.

Annual level of immigration recommended by Canadian Ethno-cultural Centre, an Ottawa-based non-profit advisory organization: 1% of the population, or approximately 250,000

Number of new immigrant students registered in Scarborough, Ont., schools between September and December 1988: 14,745

THE HOT SEAT

Conventional wisdom says the most difficult portfolio in the federal cabinet is Finance, which has to grapple with the deficit and present that annual dose of unpalatable medicine called the Budget. But Canada had just three finance ministers in the 1980s (Allan MacEachen and Marc Lalonde for the Liberals and Michael Wilson for the Conservatives), while the Department of Immigration had no less than five ministers. They were:

Lloyd Axworthy, Lib. (Mar. '80-Aug. '83)
John Roberts, Lib. (Aug. '83-Sept. '84)
Flora MacDonald, PC (Sept. '84-June '86)
Benoît Bouchard, PC (June '86-Mar. '88)
Barbara McDougall, PC (Mar. '88-present)

"To prosper, Canada must get better, not bigger."

JOHN MEYER, PAST PRESIDENT, ZERO POPULATION GROWTH, NOVEMBER 1987

"Canadian racism, like so much else in the Canadian character, is subtle, timid and, in the long run, impotent."

MORTON WEINFELD, CHAIRMAN, SOCIOLOGY DEPARTMENT, MCGILL UNIVERSITY, JUNE 1987

"That was definitely the kick that woke up the sleeping dog."

IMMIGRATION DEPARTMENT SPOKESMAN LEN WESTERBERG, ON THE INFLUENCE OF 155 TAMIL REFUGEES ARRIVING BY BOAT IN NEWFOUNDLAND ON RACIST SENTIMENT IN CANADA, DECEMBER 1985

IMMIGRATION TO CANADA, 1980-1988
Total number of immigrants: 1,067,063

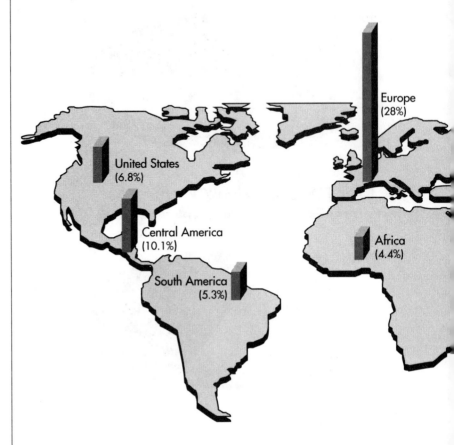

United States (6.8%)

Central America (10.1%)

South America (5.3%)

Europe (28%)

Africa (4.4%)

1981 NOV.
20,000 Canadian workers are laid off.

1982 JAN.
Ottawa requires companies to hire Canadians for any job requiring a training period of three months or less. Skilled foreigners in certain categories — mining, manufacturing and construction — are banned.

1982 NOV.
With unemployment continuing to rise, Ottawa cuts back immigration levels for 1983 by 25%.

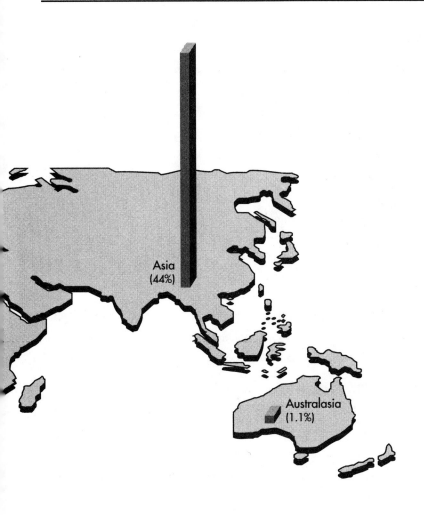

Asia
(44%)

Australasia
(1.1%)

FACTS

Percentage of the student population in Toronto and Vancouver in 1989 for whom English was a second language: 25
Estimated 1989 cost of teaching immigrants, extra English classes, psychological and social services: $10 million a year

Number of people who monthly used food banks in Metro Toronto in March 1989: 84,000
Number who were refugee claimants: 15,000

Percentage of the world's refugees who are women: 80
Percentage of refugees that Canada accepts who are women: 30

Percentage of independent corner stores owned by Koreans in Ontario in 1984: 85

1984 APRIL
A Montreal taxi company dismisses 24 Haitians on the ground that customers won't hire black drivers.

1985 APRIL
The Supreme Court of Canada says all refugee claimants are entitled to oral hearings before their applications are adjudicated.

1985 DEC.
155 Tamil refugees from Sri Lanka arrive off the coast of Newfoundland.

"There's a manifestation of certain attitudes on the part of Canadians that are far from favourable toward refugees and immigrants."

IMMIGRATION MINISTER BENOÎT BOUCHARD, AFTER 700 REFUGEES ARRIVED IN MONTREAL BETWEEN DECEMBER 25 AND 27, 1986

"There's a deep fear of the unknown, a latent racism. We've got to look at ourselves, warts and all. We can either curse the darkness or light some candles."

WALTER McLEAN, THEN MINISTER OF STATE FOR IMMIGRATION, 1985

WHAT IS IT?

THE BUSINESS IMMIGRATION PROGRAM: People with net worth of $500,000 are granted citizenship if they invest $250,000 for three years. Critics say the practice is akin to selling passports; supporters say it brings capital and creates jobs. A second category, for immigrant entrepreneurs, lowers the investment requirement to $150,000 but asks that they apply their skills to the business. In 1987, the top five source countries for business immigrants were: Hong Kong (863), South Korea (224), Taiwan (199), United States (158) and France (157). In 1985, almost 41% of all business immigrants settled in Ontario, while 26% settled in Quebec. Two years later, Ontario's portion had dropped to 32%, while Quebec's had jumped to 37.5%.

QUEUE JUMPING: When would-be immigrants come to Canada illegally and claim refugee status, they leapfrog thousands of others who have properly applied for entry visas from abroad.

THE POINT SYSTEM: Would-be immigrants to Canada gain entry on the basis of a system that awards certain kinds of professions more points than others. For example, chemists, physicists, biologists, architects, economists, and systems analysts get 1 point. Librarians and archivists get 10 points. In the medical field, doctors get no points, veterinarians get 1 point; nurses and therapists get 10 points.

1986 MARCH

The Erik Nielsen Task Force on Program Review proposes that "refugees only be selected from abroad, the number to be determined on the basis of their sponsorship by Canadians and their ability to adapt successfully to Canadian society."

1987 FEB.

New immigration rules allow officials to detain would-be refugees at the border pending a hearing.

1987 MAY

Ottawa passes Bill C-55. Aimed at accelerating the refugee process, it reduces the number of possible hearings from seven to three.

Predictably, blue-collar workers were most antagonistic to the prospect of competition in the form of skilled immigrants. Predictably, too, the hard-hit Western provinces most wanted to discourage new arrivals. In time, as job pressures eased, attitudes relaxed. By the autumn of 1987, support for skilled immigration had returned to pre-recession levels, roughly 52%.

But if Canadians are divided on the question of immigration, we are even more sharply split on the thorny issue of refugees. When asked, in September 1987, whether Canada had a moral obligation to open its doors to those fleeing persecution in their native countries, 45% agreed; 46% disagreed. (The remainder voiced no opinion.) Generally, those most sympathetic to refugees were younger (ages 25-34), single residents of Quebec, and those with post-secondary education; those least sympathetic were British Columbians, 40-to-50-year olds, and people who had not attended university. And the likelier one was to oppose open immigration, the likelier one was to deny any moral obligation to help refugees seeking sanctuary in Canada.

In fact, it is the notion of unfettered immigration that Canadians resist most, especially with respect to refugees. Canadians believe that many aspiring refugees are victims of economic deprivation, not genuine targets of political persecution. Admitting them as refugees is considered an abuse of the system.

But we are also wary of the social consequences of too liberal immigration policies. In the fall of 1987, 54% said new immigrants weren't willing to adapt to the Canadian way of doing things. Some 48% said they were uncomfortable with the way Canadian society was changing as a result of immigration. And 49% said bluntly that too many people from different races and cultures had been allowed to live in Canada. The same question, asked in the summer of 1989, elicited only marginally different responses.

Our thinking on these questions is logical. Those who voice discomfort with the way immigration is changing the character of Canada – the less affluent, the elderly, union members, and residents of smaller communities – are likeliest to see problems with the diverse ethnic make-up of immigrants and their willingness to assimilate. Naturally, they are also likelier to oppose open immigration.

FACTS

Number of immigrants to Canada from Hong Kong in 1988: 24,588
Number of Hong Kong Chinese applying for visas in the Canadian Commission office in June 1989, after the massacre of Chinese students in Beijing's Tiananmen Square: 9,000 a day

Between 1956 and 1962, only 8% of immigrants to Canada came from countries other than the United States or the European nations. Since 1977, 60% have come from non-traditional source countries. In the next decade, that portion is expected to rise to 70%.

"First and foremost, you have to recognize, accept and be proud of the fact that this country is composed of people who are very compassionate and who have always seen immigration as being a major factor in the development of the country."

IMMIGRATION MINISTER FLORA MacDONALD, DECEMBER 1984

"I am continuing the restriction on selected workers from abroad to protect jobs for Canadians."

IMMIGRATION MINISTER JOHN ROBERTS, NOVEMBER 1983, AFTER CANADA'S UNEMPLOYMENT RATE WENT TO 11.8%

And while Canadians generally agree that governments should provide more aid to the truly needy, recent immigrants apparently don't fit that description. Throughout the 1980s, Canadians ringingly endorsed giving greater government assistance to the poor, the elderly, and the unemployed. But no more than 28% ever favoured offering more help to immigrants. In fact, more of us wanted government aid to immigrants reduced than wanted it increased.

One could fairly conclude that a significant portion of the Canadian population is uncomfortable with not just the idea of freer immigration but with the very notion of multiculturalism – one of the bedrock building blocks of the modern Canadian mosaic. We salute the abstraction; we seem to resent the reality. And the persistence of these attitudes through the 1980s, in times of economic wellbeing as well as of hardship, strongly suggests they aren't going to change for some time – if ever.

INTO THE NINETIES

Canada averaged as few as 75,000 net immigrants a year in the mid-1980s. The evidence suggests that we must get to 200,000 a year by the 1990s. The reasons are obvious. The baby boom has produced no ancillary echo, so there will be fewer workers. The impact of female participation in the workforce, driven by education, is a critical factor; it has had a significant dampening effect on fertility rates. In combination, these trends suggest that the prospect for a population shortfall in the 1990s is almost certain. The only way Canada can have a growing population – the prima facie prerequisite of a healthy economy – is through immigration.

It is also clear that this immigration is going to come from countries it has come from for the past twenty-five years – and from countries it never came from before. From 1905-67, 85% of all immigrants came from Europe and America; these nations now account for less than 25%. Today, our immigration comes largely from Asia, Africa, the West Indies, the Third World – the first wave of visible-minority immigration in Canadian history. Given world economic conditions and pressures, it seems inescapable that Canada will become blacker in the 1990s than it has ever been before.

FILLING THE QUOTA

Projected immigration for 1980:	120,000
Actual immigration:	143,117
Projected immigration for 1981:	130,000-140,000
Actual immigration:	128,618
Projected immigration for 1982:	130,000-135,000
Actual immigration:	121,147
Projected immigration for 1983:	105,000-110,000
Actual immigration:	89,157
Projected immigration for 1984:	90,000-95,000
Actual immigration:	88,239
Projected immigration for 1985:	85,000-90,000
Actual immigration:	84,303
Projected immigration for 1986:	105,000-115,000
Actual immigration:	99,219
Projected immigration for 1987:	125,000
Actual immigration:	152,098
Projected immigration for 1988:	125,000-135,000
Actual immigration:	159,437
Projected immigration for 1989:	150,000-160,000
Actual immigration:	190,000 (unofficial estimate)
Projected immigration for 1990:	165,000-175,000

FACTS

Number of immigrants admitted to Canada under the entrepreneur category in 1983: 1,982
Amount of money they brought with them: $820 million
Number of jobs they created: 4,600
Number admitted in the same category in 1987: 3,128
Amount of money they brought with them: $3.1 billion
Number of jobs they created: 11,918
According to a 1985 federal survey, 40% of the entrepreneurs granted landed-immigrant status have disappeared; they cannot be located anywhere in the country.

Net immigration to Canada in 1985: 36,000
Net immigration in 1989: 75,000

1987 AUG.
174 East Indians, mostly Sikhs from the Punjab, come ashore on the southwest coast of Nova Scotia. Parliament is recalled from summer recess to pass emergency legislation aimed at preventing further illegal arrivals.

1988 JULY
Ottawa changes the rules governing the family-class immigration category, allowing easier entry for children of immigrants who have become Canadian citizens or permanent residents.

1989 JAN.
Ottawa's new immigration law sets criteria for granting refugee status and proposes penalties for those who help unauthorized refugees to come to Canada.

"You're not helping a lot of people if you bring them in but can't give them the kind of support they need."

IMMIGRATION MINISTER LLOYD AXWORTHY, OCTOBER 1982, EXPLAINING WHY CANADA WAS CUTTING THE NUMBER OF INDEPENDENT WORKERS IT WOULD ACCEPT FROM ABROAD

"At a guess, this has been true since the Montagnais-Naskapi watched de Champlain drop anchor off Quebec City in 1608."

MICHAEL VALPY OF THE *GLOBE AND MAIL*, COMMENTING ON POLLS SHOWING A MAJORITY OF CANADIANS THINK CANADA ACCEPTS TOO MANY IMMIGRANTS, MARCH 1989

"Send them buggers back."

ELMER KNUTSEN, LEADER OF THE CONFEDERATION OF REGIONS PARTY, ON THE ISSUE OF ILLEGAL IMMIGRATION, JANUARY 1989

IMMIGRATION BY PROVINCE OF INTENDED DESTINATION, 1980-1988

Total number of immigrants: 1,067,063

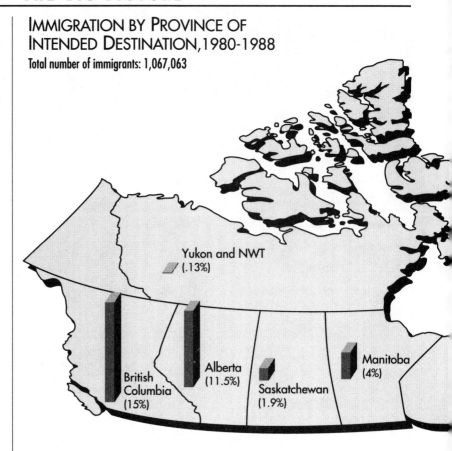

Yukon and NWT (.13%)

British Columbia (15%)

Alberta (11.5%)

Saskatchewan (1.9%)

Manitoba (4%)

UNEASY PASSAGE   A boatload of Tamils arrived in Newfoundland without visas in August 1986. The debate about their admission ignited a controversy over immigration policy.

1989 MAY
Immigration Minister Barbara McDougall appeals to Rotarians and Kiwanians to "help stem the growing tide of racism in our country."

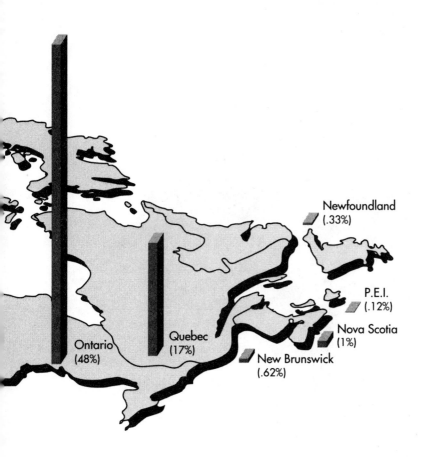

Newfoundland
(.33%)

P.E.I.
(.12%)

Nova Scotia
(1%)

New Brunswick
(.62%)

Ontario
(48%)

Quebec
(17%)

FACTS

In 1986, Canada's non-white population stood at 1,600,000. That figure represented just 6.4% of the total population. If 70% of all immigration between now and 2001 were non-white, Canada's total non-white population would not exceed 9.6%.

In 1987, 56% of all immigrants to Canada settled in Ontario. Of those settling in Ontario, 6 of 10 took residence in Toronto.

Percentage of Canada's male population that has university degrees: 9.9
Of women: 6.2
Percentage of non-white male immigrants who have university degrees: 20.8
Of non-white women: 12.7

THE SOUND OF RACISM
With the underdeveloped countries of the Third World accounting for more than 60 percent of the country's immigration, Canadians confronted prejudices in the 1980s they once considered other people's problems.

"We need immigration rates that are consistent with our absorptive capacity, without dramatically changing the nature of Canada itself."

KIM ABBOTT, FOUNDER OF THE IMMIGRATION ASSOCIATION OF CANADA, JANUARY 1989

"For years now, you [Parliament] have been keeping white folk out and letting every other SOB in. It's all the same to you if we wind up wearing loin cloths."

VANCOUVER COLUMNIST DOUG COLLINS, WHO RAN UNSUCCESSFULLY IN THE 1988 FEDERAL ELECTION FOR THE REFORM PARTY OF CANADA AND RECOMMENDED A RETURN TO IMMIGRATION POLICIES OF THE 1950S AND 1960S, WHEN NON-WHITE IMMIGRATION WAS REGULATED BY STRICT QUOTAS, AUTUMN 1988

UNEMPLOYMENT AND IMMIGRATION

What is the most important problem facing Canada today—in other words, the one that concerns you personally the most?

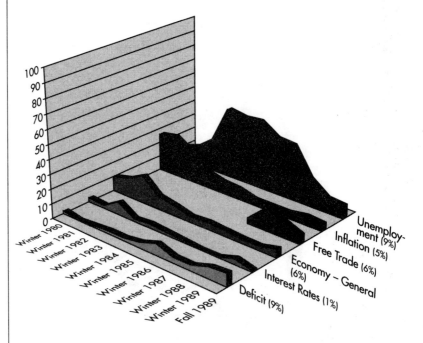

The recession of the early eighties drove concerns about unemployment to record highs. In response, Ottawa shut the immigration doors.

WHAT PRICE ADMISSION   Some Canadians called the Tamils who landed off the coast of Newfoundland political refugees. Others, however, saw them as economic opportunists and urged their immediate deportation.

From time to time, we will hear quiet, private, almost anguished pleas for more immigration from Europe, especially now that the Berlin Wall is down and the borders of Eastern Europe are open. The very plea is symptomatic of an underlying racism. But with 1992 in the offing, the most attractive destination for East Europeans will be Western Europe. For the first time since the Napoleonic era, Europe is expressing its sense of continent – and its confidence. The epicentre of economic power is returning to Europe.

As Canadians, we revel in our multicultural traditions. But one doesn't have to scratch very deep to find racist sentiments at work. Canadians make a distinction between immigration that has occurred to date, which is spiritually uplifting, and immigration that will occur in the future, which is not. And those who are most reluctant to accept more immigration tend to be the children of immigrants. They believe there was something noble about their parents' entry into Canada, but they refuse to ascribe the same nobility to new arrivals. The difference, of course, is that they were white; the new wave is almost entirely coloured.

As they did in the 1980s, immigrants in the 1990s will settle principally in the cities, adding to pressures that some Canadians already feel to flee to the suburbs and rural environs. To some extent, Canada will experience what Americans have grown accustomed to – black or non-white inner cities, white suburbia and countrysides. Already, one can see changes in patterns of intra-city migration. In the 1990s whole communities will change complexion. There will be shifting demands on employers and governments, and questions about their proper role. Growing social unrest and racism in this peaceable kingdom are not unlikely.

Despite these racial tensions, we will continue to attract an extraordinarily high calibre of immigrant. The average net worth of immigrants now arriving in Canada is $25,000 more than the average net worth of those already here. This is no accident. Only the affluent can afford to escape from their native countries. And our point and quota systems demand asset and education levels that only the affluent can meet. This entrepreneurial class tends to do well economically – too well for some Canadians. While other Canadians grapple with the economy, the environment, civic affairs, etc., the immigrants apply themselves to their work,

FACTS

Number of refugee welfare cases on the rolls of Ontario's Peel Regional Council in the summer of 1986: 5
Number in February, 1987, after Ottawa required refugee claimants to wait for status to get special permits: 56

In 1871, Canada's population was 61% British, 31% French, 7% other European and 1% visible minorities – i.e. non-white. By 1986, the composition had changed dramatically: 34% British, 24% French, 20% multiple countries of origin; 22% other. Between 1980 and 1986, immigrants from Africa, Asia, and Latin America made up 65% of the total.

"We see this basically as an almost uncontrolled invasion. We should be worried [not about whether our children will speak French or English but] about whether they'll speak Chinese or Hindi."

PAUL FROMM, OF THE RIGHT-WING CITIZENS FOR FOREIGN AID REFORM, JANUARY 1989, ON CURRENT LEVELS OF IMMIGRATION. IN THE 1988 FEDERAL ELECTION, FROMM RAN UNDER THE BANNER OF THE CONFEDERATION OF REGIONS PARTY IN THE RIDING OF MISSISSAUGA EAST. HE WON 257 VOTES, ABOUT 1% OF THE NUMBER CAST FOR THE WINNER, LIBERAL ALBINA GUARNIERI.

"The more distant a culture is from our own, the more gradual the number of people from it you let in at one time."

BARBARA AMIEL, IN *MACLEAN'S*, MAY 1984

THE SHAPE OF THE FUTURE

For several years, Canada's fertility rate – the number of children to whom the average woman could be expected to give birth – has been roughly 1.7. But any fertility rate below 2.1 will not – in the absence of immigration – yield enough births to replace the population. If the current fertility rate were maintained, and if immigration were to continue at roughly 130,000 per year, Canada's population would peak at 31 million in 2026 and then begin a steady decline, stabilizing at 18 million 700 years from now. If immigration were to rise to 200,000, the population would peak at 35 million and gradually decline modestly to 33 million. Whatever the levels of immigration, some analysts think fertility rates will actually decline over the next decade, casting doubt on the accuracy of these projections. Indeed, if fertility ratios were to fall to 1.4, and immigration were to run at 185,000 a year, the population in the year 2050 would be 25 million, less than it is today.

MORE OR LESS?

In 1988, about 160,000 immigrants were allowed into Canada. Over the next decade, how many should be admitted each year?

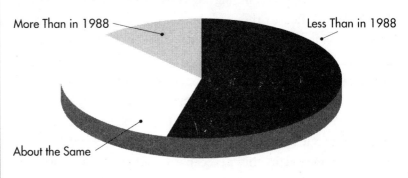

More Than in 1988

Less Than in 1988

About the Same

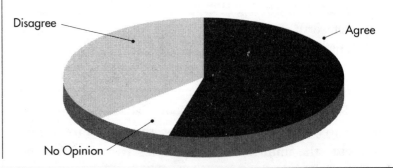

Disagree

Agree

No Opinion

starting businesses, buying real estate, making money. Their success breeds resentment.

By and large, immigrants in the 1990s will want what immigrants to Canada have always wanted: a better, more secure life. But racism will make it more difficult to attain. The newly arrived Haitian knows he will never become president of the Royal Bank of Canada, but his son or his grandson may. There will be pressure on the sons and daughters of first-generation Canadians to adopt the mores of the host culture. And there will be a counter-pressure on their parents not to become completely isolated or irrelevant. The easiest way to do that is to become active in their own community – to seek legitimacy from within.

The new immigrants will use their voting power to accelerate integration, to gain access to the system and lower the barriers to acceptance. In the Liberal Party, ethnic groups have begun to take control of the constituency-level party machinery, and more will do so in the decade ahead. They will make greater strides in the political arena than in the business world, although that, too, will come in time.

The multicultural ethos of the 1970s – the desire to maintain, encourage and glorify ethno-cultural differences – will shift as well. Jamaicans don't need to be told that they have a rich heritage. What they need is tolerance; they want their white neighbour to stop calling them niggers. Within the immigrant communities, there will be sharp debate about how to win tolerance and shorten the process of absorption. Some will argue that drawing attention to the problem of racism only raises the ire of the host culture. Others will say that you can't change attitudes by telling Canadians that blacks are just like whites; you can only change attitudes by forcing changes in behaviour through legislation. Rights must be codified.

But what will make the 1990s unique in immigration terms is that for the first time since 1905, when Clifford Sifton populated Western Canada, immigration policy will become economic policy instead of social policy – a lever to be pulled to replenish what otherwise would be a stagnant and shrinking population. No political leader in Canada is yet prepared to advocate this notion, but economic realities will make it inevitable. As the decade passes, the pressure will increase and the doors will open wide, with profound political and social consequences for all Canadians.

FACTS

In 1950, when immigration to Canada was 60,000, unemployment stood at 1.75%.
In 1951, when immigration jumped to 200,000, the unemployment rate fell to 1.25%.

Canadians opposed to immigration sometimes argue that opening the door too wide will lead to overcrowding – and to the social problems that often ensue.
In fact, Canada has one of the lowest population densities in the industrialized world.
Canada: 26 people per square kilometre
United States: 30
France: 100
Denmark: 119
Italy: 188
United Kingdom: 231
West Germany: 247
Japan: 318
Netherlands: 427

OUTWARD BOUND

CHAPTER 10

"There will be no veterans of World War III."

WALTER MONDALE

"It is not of Communism that we should be afraid, but rather of the fact that people are starving to death."

PIERRE TRUDEAU

CANADIANS HAVE LONG BEEN REGARDED AS AN INSULAR PEOPLE, too preoccupied with the business of domestic survival to pay much attention to the world at large. What happened elsewhere, we assumed, had minimal impact on our lives. What happened at home, we knew, had no impact on the world beyond our borders. Our introversion was so deeply rooted that most people, at least until the mid-1980s, believed that inflation, interest rates, and other economic malaises were entirely domestic problems – as if the policies set by central banks in London, Washington, and Tokyo did not touch us.

The events of the 1980s stripped away that protective cocoon. The escalation of nuclear tensions in the early 1980s; war in the Falkland Islands and Grenada; famine in Africa; the wanton destruction of Air India Flight 182 and other passenger jets by shadowy terrorists; the emergence of Mikhail Gorbachev; the collapse of Communism in Eastern Europe; and the continuing dilemmas posed by living next to the earth's pre-eminent superpower – all of this and more impinged on the national psyche. If Canada did not affect the world, the world certainly affected Canada.

FRAGMENTS OF TERROR   The bombing of an Air India passenger jet over the Atlantic in 1985 demonstrated to Canadians that they were no more immune to the horrors of political extremism than any other nation.

"We are living in a new era. International airports are literally world crossroads, and many old scores and new scores can be settled."

TRANSPORT MINISTER DON MAZANKOWSKI, ORDERING TIGHTER SECURITY AT CANADIAN AIRPORTS IN THE WAKE OF THE 1985 BOMBING OF AIR INDIA FLIGHT 182

It was not simply that television made everything more accessible. It was also that global events themselves increasingly seemed to have a measurable impact on Canadian life. Hence, Washington's 1983 request to test the unarmed cruise missile over Canadian terrain provoked debate about our own commitment to the North Atlantic Treaty Organization. Was saying yes tantamount to surrendering sovereignty and an escalation of the arms race? Or was it a statement of allegiance to the cause of world peace? And what was Canada's proper role in NATO? Similarly, the bombs that blew up one Air India flight in 1985 and nearly a second signalled all too clearly that terrorism was not only something that occurred somewhere else – in the Middle East or the airports of Europe; Canadians, too, could be victimized by the private wars of determined terrorists. And the fact that in 1997 Great Britain's lease of Hong Kong would come to an end set off a mini-avalanche of emigration to Canada. The newcomers brought a pool of talent and money, affecting everything from jobs to housing.

Throughout the decade, two major topics dominated Canadian thinking about the world: global security (the arms race, disarmament, the threat of nuclear war); and famine and hunger in the Third World. But while 40% said poverty and hunger were the world's most serious problems, only 20% thought they were a foreign-policy priority of the Canadian government. And although 28% called reducing the threat of war the top global concern, only 18% said it was number one on Ottawa's agenda. In fact in one 1985 survey, the largest number of respondents (38%) said the government's chief foreign-policy thrust was directed at trade and other economic issues – a subject only 20% identified as the most critical problem. Not surprisingly, more than three in four Canadians wanted to correct this imbalance, by having Ottawa increase efforts to improve East-West relations, lower the level of armaments, and reduce hunger.

Most of us (77%) were hopeful that such policies would influence the world. We saw Canada as a politically stable, peaceful, industrial power – respected for its relative neutrality on global issues; 67% said other nations regarded Canada as a mediator and a peacekeeper. Ottawa could gain even more influence in world councils, Canadians maintained, by stressing our trade and economic power, by speaking out more often on international issues

ASSASSINATIONS IN THE EIGHTIES

1980: Liberian President William Tolbert; Nicaraguan President Anastasio Somoza Debayle

1981: U.S. President Ronald Reagan (unsuccessful attempt); Egyptian President Anwar Sadat; Iranian President Mohammed Ali Raji and Premier Mohammed Jad Bahonar; Bangladeshi President Ziaur Rahman; Pope John Paul II (unsuccessful attempt)

1982: Lebanon's president-elect Bashir Gemayel

1983: Filipino opposition leader Benigno Aquino, Jr.; four cabinet ministers in the South Korean government; Grenadian Prime Minister Maurice Bishop (executed)

1984: Indian Prime Minister Indira Gandhi; British Prime Minister Margaret Thatcher (unsuccessful attempt)

1986: Swedish Prime Minister Olof Palme

1987: Lebanese Premier Rashid Karami

1988: PLO military leader Khalil Wazir; Pakistan President Mohammed Zia ul Haq (presumed)

1989: Romanian President Nicolae Ceausescu (executed)

FACTS

Canadian government spending on defence in 1980: $4.375 billion
Percentage of government spending that represented: 8.6
Spending on defence in 1988: $10.34 billion
Percentage of government spending that represented: 9.4

Size of Canada's defence budget in 1989-90: $11.2 billion
Amount spent in Europe's defence: $1.2 billion

1980 JAN.

Canada's ambassador to Iran, Ken Taylor, orchestrates the escape from Iran of six U.S. diplomats using false Canadian passports.

1980 APRIL

Ottawa announces that it will not participate in the 1980 summer Olympic Games in Moscow, in protest against the Soviet invasion of Afghanistan in December 1979.

1981 MAY

The North American Air Defense Command, of which Canada is a member, officially becomes the North American Aerospace Defense Command, reflecting the alliance's new interest in space weaponry.

"Gentlemen, we really do have a very porous system."

MAJOR-GENERAL LAWRENCE ASHLEY, TESTIFYING BEFORE A HOUSE OF COMMONS COMMITTEE ON THE NEED TO MODERNIZE CANADA'S DISTANT EARLY WARNING (DEW) LINE, 1985

TERRORISTS OF THE EIGHTIES

FRANCE: Action Directe

GERMANY: The Baader Meinhof Gang

GREECE: Organization 17 November

ITALY: The Red Brigades

JAPAN: The Japanese Red Army

SPAIN: Basque Fatherland and Liberty (ETA)

BRITAIN: The Irish Republican Army

COLOMBIA: M-19 and the National Liberation Army (ELN)

PERU: Sendero Luminoso (Shining Path)

SYRIA: The Popular Front for the Liberation of Palestine

IRAN: Hezbollah (Party of God)

GUATEMALA: The UNRG, an umbrella organization of four left-wing groups

EL SALVADOR: The FDR-FMLN, a left-wing coalition of revolutionary organizations

NICARAGUA: The Contras, a coalition of right-wing anti-Sandinista military units

SRI LANKA: The Liberation Tigers of Tamil Eelam

INDIA: Sikh Dashmesh (10th) Regiment

ARMENIA: The Armenian Secret Army for the Liberation of Armenia

WESTERN SAHARA: Polisario Front

1981 JUNE

Canada hosts the summit of the world's seven leading industrialized countries in Montebello, Quebec.

1981 NOV.

U.S.-Soviet discussions on limiting intermediate-range nuclear forces (INF) in Europe begin in Geneva. Six years later, Mikhail Gorbachev and Ronald Reagan sign an INF treaty in Washington, eliminating medium- and short-range nuclear weapons.

1982 NOV.

Defence Minister Gilles Lamontagne defends Ottawa's purchase of 138 CF-18 fighter jets for $4.9 billion. The cost and the choice are controversial. By April 1990, 13 CF-18s have crashed, and seven pilots have died.

THE THREAT OF NUCLEAR WAR

How likely is it that there will be a nuclear confrontation or war in our lifetime?

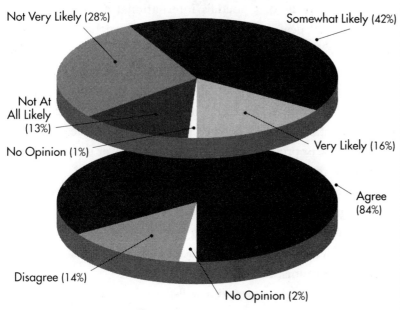

Not Very Likely (28%)

Somewhat Likely (42%)

Not At All Likely (13%)

No Opinion (1%)

Very Likely (16%)

Agree (84%)

Disagree (14%)

No Opinion (2%)

It isn't possible to have a limited nuclear war

FACTS

Size of Canadian armed forces in 1970: 93,353 Size of armed forces in 1989: 86,261

Canada's contribution to the North Atlantic Treaty Organization in 1988: $12 billion The percentage of NATO's total budget this represented: 2 Italy's contribution to NATO: $20.4 billion

1982 DEC.

Canada and 118 other nations become signatories to the Law of the Sea Convention, which recognizes the Canadian claim to a 200-mile off-shore economic zone, among other things.

1983 FEB.

Ottawa reaches agreement with Washington on the testing of U.S. military equipment in Canada, including the cruise missile. Testing begins in March 1984.

1983 SEPT.

The Soviet Union shoots down Korean Airlines Flight 007, killing 269 people, including 10 Canadians. Ottawa subsequently claims $2.1 million in compensation for families of the Canadian victims.

"The problem is not so much Canadian secrets. Most adversaries know the state of Canada's armed forces. It is the possible access to material from the NATO alliance available to Canada. Canada is known as potentially easy picking grounds."

PAUL HELLYER, FORMER LIBERAL DEFENSE MINISTER, COMMENTING ON THE RESIGNATION OF CONSERVATIVE DEFENSE MINISTER ROBERT COATES, AFTER HE VISITED A STRIP CLUB IN LAHR, WEST GERMANY, 1985

and by spending more on aid to developing countries. (Those who minimized the influence of Canadian foreign policy cited our lack of military strength, our small population, and our domination by the United States.)

The genesis of Canada's international awakening in the 1980s was the peace issue. Specifically, it was a debate about modernizing NATO's nuclear missiles in Europe, about the Soviet Union's lethal SS-20s, about letting the Americans test cruise missiles over Canada, and about Star Wars, the pejorative name that came to be given to Washington's Strategic Defense Initiative. Fundamentally, it was a debate about whether defence build-ups would cause or prevent the next world war – a war that threatened to kill not only millions of people, but life itself. Canadians were deeply concerned about this issue. In fact, 84% of Decima respondents agreed in 1983 that there was no such thing as a "limited" nuclear war; 58% thought such a war was likely in their lifetime; and in November 1987, 60% said they would rather live under Soviet Communist rule than risk nuclear war.

Still, most of us viewed a well-prepared army as something that helped to keep the peace. Some 47% said Ottawa did not spend enough on defence; 73% recognized that Canada spent less (or significantly less) on defence than other countries its size; three out of four respondents said it was important for Canada to maintain a large, strong military force. And 57% agreed that in the absence of wholesale disarmament, the policy of mutual assured destruction – based on the ability of the United States and the Soviet Union to inflict intolerable damage on each other in any confrontation – would help deter nuclear war.

But our principles were often affected by practical considerations. When asked to weigh defence spending against other government programs such as social services, only 25% thought Ottawa should allocate more to the military; 36% said more should be spent on other services; and 36% said the present division of capital was well balanced. While an overwhelming 89% supported Canada's participation in NATO, the population was evenly split – 49% in favour, 50% against – on the question of letting Washington use Canada to test the cruise missile. A similar split was evident on the Strategic Defense Initiative, the U.S. plan to erect a system of land- and space-based weapons that could destroy enemy missiles in flight.

WARS OF THE EIGHTIES

AFGHANISTAN: 1979-89: The Soviet Union and Afghanistan's Communist government versus a coalition of U.S.-backed Afghan rebels. In 1989, the Soviet Union effectively concedes defeat and withdraws its troops, leaving Afghanistan in civil war.

IRAN-IRAQ: In September 1980, Iraq declares war on Iran, only months after the succession of the Ayatollah Ruholla Khomeini. The war lasts eight years and kills an estimated one million people.

FALKLAND ISLANDS: In April 1982, Argentina declares war on Great Britain and invades the Falklands (Malvinas). The war lasts less than three months. Britain is the victor. The loss of the war discredits Argentina's military leadership, and leads to the restoration of democracy.

LIBYA-CHAD: In June 1982, the rebel forces of Hissen Habre oust the Libyan-backed government. With help from France, Habre gradually repulses Libyan troops.

GRENADA: In October 1983, the United States invades the Caribbean island, topples a Marxist government, and restores democracy. The war lasts less than a week.

PANAMA: American troops invade in May 1989, overthrowing Panamanian strongman Manuel Noriega.

FACTS

Percentage of gross national product Canada spent on defence between 1983 and 1987: 2.17
Percentage spent by the United States: 5.98
Percentage spent by Greece: 6.52
Percentage spent by Great Britain: 5.01
Percentage spent by West Germany: 3.2
Percentage spent by Belgium: 3.26
Only NATO nations that spent less than Canada: Italy and Luxemburg

1983 NOV.

Prime Minister Pierre Trudeau embarks on a self-proclaimed peace mission to end the nuclear-arms race, visiting dozens of world leaders over a four-month period. Although the Trudeau mission did not succeed, it won him the Albert Einstein Peace Prize in 1984.

1984 APRIL

The Canadian Institute for International Peace and Security is formed in Ottawa.

1984 OCT.

Famine breaks out in Ethiopia. Television crews film the skeletal survivors of relief camps. David MacDonald, a former Conservative cabinet minister, is named Canada's Emergency Co-ordinator.

"Let's face it. This is as close as we will ever get to actually doing what we were trained to do."

EDWARD DAVIDSON, WARRANT OFFICER, CANADIAN ARMED FORCES, ON TAKING UP PEACE-KEEPING DUTIES IN IRAQ, 1988

LONG-RUNNING WARS

LEBANON: The nation's warring factions – Christian, Muslim, Druse, Armenian – continued the civil war that began in 1975, often fighting among themselves. The Israelis intervened in 1982 but withdrew in failure. The Americans came as well, only to retreat after a suicide attack on a Marine base in Beirut in 1983 killed 237 soldiers. Syrian troops imposed order, but it was punctuated by car bombs, assassinations, kidnappings of foreigners and, quite frequently, full-scale fighting.

CAMBODIA (KAMPUCHEA): Soviet-backed Vietnamese troops, which had invaded in 1978, continued to fight a coalition of anti-Soviet forces for the better part of the decade. But the Vietnamese began withdrawing in 1989, leaving the political future of Cambodia unresolved.

SOMALIA-ETHIOPIA: In a war for control of the Ogaden, an eastern province of Ethiopia, fighting continues until a 1988 peace treaty is signed.

NATIONS THAT WENT DEMOCRATIC IN THE 80'S

Brazil (1985), Argentina (1983), Peru (1980), Uruguay (1985), Chile (1989), Grenada (1983), Honduras (1982), Nepal (1986), Nicaragua (1990), Panama (1989), Poland (1989), East Germany (1989), Czechoslovakia (1989), Hungary (1989), Romania (1989), South Korea (1987), Surinam (1988), Turkey (1983)

1985 MARCH

Three Armenian terrorists seize the Turkish embassy in Ottawa, killing a Pinkerton security guard. It is the third Armenian attack on Turkish diplomats since 1982.

1985 JUNE

Air India Flight 182 blows up en route from Toronto to London, killing 329 passengers and crew. Sikh terrorists are implicated.

1986 NOV.

Ronald Reagan and Mikhail Gorbachev hold their first summit meeting, in Geneva.

NATO: ALLY OR ORPHAN?

Does Canada contribute more than its fair share, its fair share, or less than its fair share to NATO?

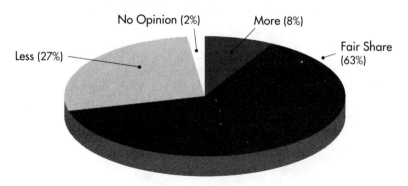

No Opinion (2%)

More (8%)

Less (27%)

Fair Share (63%)

SHOULD CANADA BELONG TO NATO?

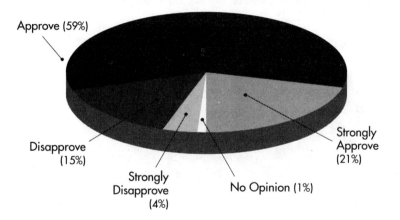

Approve (59%)

Disapprove (15%)

Strongly Disapprove (4%)

No Opinion (1%)

Strongly Approve (21%)

FACTS

NATO's total budget in 1989-90: $300 billion
Percentage accounted for by the United States: 50

Percentage of gross national product Canadian companies spent on research and development in 1989: 1.3
Percentage spent by United States firms: 2.6
Percentage spent in Japan: 2.9

1986 JUNE

The minister of defence, Perrin Beatty, releases a long-awaited white paper that recommends the building of 10 to 12 nuclear-powered submarines for use in the Arctic. The submarines subsequently fall victim to budget cuts.

1986 DEC.

Ronald Reagan and Mikhail Gorbachev meet again, in Reykjavik, Iceland.

1987 SEPT.

Canada plays host to La Francophonie, a summit of the world's French-speaking nations in Quebec City.

BANG FOR THE BUCK

Does Canada spend too much, about the right amount, or too little on the military and defence?

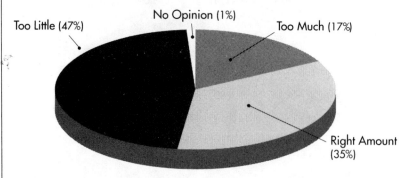

Too Little (47%)

No Opinion (1%)

Too Much (17%)

Right Amount (35%)

Should we put a greater emphasis on defence spending, a greater emphasis on other kinds of spending like social services, or do you think we currently have the right balance between defence and other types of spending?

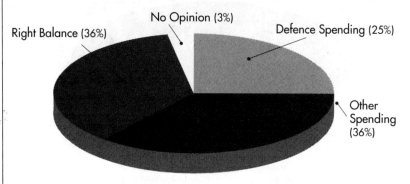

Right Balance (36%)

No Opinion (3%)

Defence Spending (25%)

Other Spending (36%)

1987 OCT.

Canada hosts the Commonwealth heads of government meeting in Vancouver.

1988 MARCH

The Department of External Affairs releases "Sharing Our Future," calling for greater emphasis on human rights in deciding which countries will receive aid, and a reduction in "tied aid," which requires recipients to use some portion of funds to buy Canadian goods and services.

1988 APRIL

Canada agrees to spend $1.2 billion as a partner in a U.S.-sponsored multinational space station.

Those who opposed SDI, like those who opposed the cruise-missile tests, said it would fuel the arms race. Those who supported the Reagan initiative considered it a deterrent. As always, a strain of traditional Canadian pragmatism was also apparent. If Star Wars were going to be built anyway, 64% said Canada should participate – and earn the technological dividend.

Our reservations about new weapons reflected our ambivalence about the United States itself. Washington was considered twice as sincere about ending the arms race as was Moscow. And 50% thought the Soviets were stronger militarily. But Canadians weren't at all convinced that adding to America's missile arsenal would increase our safety from nuclear conflict. And only one in four respondents believed Ottawa should follow the U.S. lead on foreign- and defence-policy matters; 75% wanted Canada to make its own decisions. While withholding majority support on the cruise issue, Canadians saluted Pierre Trudeau's 1983 peace and disarmament campaign; 85% endorsed the prime minister's mission – although only 50% thought he had any chance of succeeding. Indeed, two out of three people surveyed said the arms race would end only when the superpowers agreed that it should end; applying world pressure, as Trudeau was attempting to do, was wasted effort.

The final Trudeau years were marked by cool relations with the United States and disputes over Canadian energy and foreign-investment policies. The election of the Mulroney government in September 1984 brought a distinct warming trend. It was a thaw Canadians welcomed. In 1985, for example, 77% endorsed closer ties with Washington; in 1981, the figure was just 64%. But, as in all things, we favoured moderation. Asked to define the ideal Canadian-U.S. relationship, the largest number (47%) said "businesslike but neighbourly."

The big picture of the early 1980s, then, reveals a Canada increasingly fearful about the prospect of nuclear war, and uncertain how to respond. But as the years passed, the international climate improved, and so too did Canadian estimates of the threat. In 1987, one year after the second Reagan-Gorbachev summit in Reykjavik, 42% said the risk of war had diminished. At home, the thaw in the Cold War manifested itself in attitudes to Ottawa's long-awaited White Paper on defence

FACTS

Rank of Canada among contributors to the United Nations: 5

Canada's ambassadors to the United Nations in the 1980s: Michel Dupuy: May 1980 - July 1981 Gérard Pelletier: August 1981 - November 1984 Stephen Lewis: December 1984 - July 1988 Yves Fortier: August 1988 to present

"We get less attention down there than Cuba, Nicaragua, El Salvador, you name it. To get a mention down in Washington, you either have to be Wayne Gretzky or a good snow storm."

PRIME MINISTER BRIAN MULRONEY, 1985

policy, released in June 1987. The basic thrust of the paper – to increase the size of the Canadian armed forces – was endorsed by only a slim majority of respondents. And support for spending more on the military dropped from 47% in 1983 to 37% in 1987 and again to 29% in December 1989. By more than a two-to-one ratio, respondents said money now spent on military research would be better spent on developing non-military technologies. Nevertheless, the public's fundamental commitment to NATO did not change significantly. Some 80% continued to endorse our membership in NATO; only 16% wanted Canada to withdraw from the alliance.

The stunning events of 1989 in Eastern Europe – the collapse of the Berlin Wall and the nascent democratization of the Warsaw Bloc nations – confirmed these trends. A large majority (72%) regarded the changes in Europe as real and lasting; the same percentage said war was less likely as a result. But a healthy measure of cynicism and skepticism remained. Canadians said the political changes sprang more from Gorbachev's need to appease public opinion than from any genuine commitment to democratic values. And 60% said Ottawa should not cut its defence budgets until there was more evidence that the changes in Europe were permanent. Nor were we prepared to make sacrifices at home to rebuild the economies of Poland and Czechoslovakia; 66% said assembling a major economic-aid package for Eastern Europe would waste taxpayers' money.

Most people believed Canada's foreign-policy effort should be directed at international trade. That 94% of Canadians supported the idea of free trade with the United States in 1984 reflected an understanding that the old protectionist parochialism would not suffice in the late 20th century. Instinctively, Canadians recognized the need to reach out and be part of the global community – or forever be left behind. The status quo had no status. In 1984, the federal Conservatives tapped this well of optimism to build a coalition for change and a parliamentary majority.

At its core, the free-trade debate was about whether Canadians were ready to compete with the world or not. Out of necessity as much as ambition, most of us were. In 1985, 77% agreed that Canada's standard of living would be seriously threatened if "we don't get a lot better at producing world-class goods and services."

THE OTTAWA-WASHINGTON AXIS

Are relations between Canada and the United States better, worse, or about the same as they were two years ago?

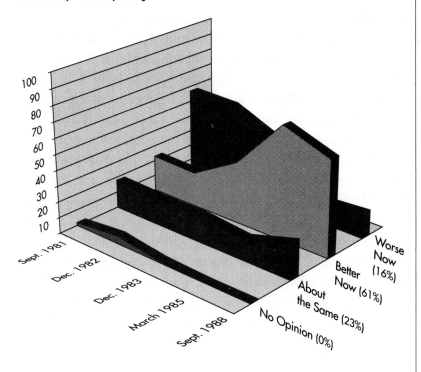

FACTS

Number of countries in which Canada maintains diplomatic, consular, or other official representation: 86

Annual program budget for the department of external affairs in 1980-81: $1.82 billion
Annual budget in 1989-90: $3.198 billion
Portion that was allocated to foreign aid (the Canadian International Development Agency and other programs) in 1980-81: $1.291 billion
In 1989-90: $1.918 billion

1988 APRIL

Ottawa announces that Canadian soldiers will act as observers in the withdrawal of Soviet troops from Afghanistan.

1988 JUNE

Canada hosts the annual meeting of the Economic Summit of industrialized nations in Toronto.

1988 AUG.

Canada sends 500 troops to the Persian Gulf, as part of a United Nations peace-keeping force.

And 66% said Ottawa should not cut its export loan and subsidy programs in order to cut the deficit. But while 64% said increasing trade should be a major foreign-policy priority, only 41% thought the federal government was doing a good job at it.

Our views on foreign aid are equally clear cut. A majority believes that current aid budgets are adequate and at least somewhat effective. Most Canadians appreciate that helping the Third World gain self-sufficiency is a moral obligation – and a long-term project; 44% think it will take between 11 and 20 years. And most respondents want Canadian aid dollars directed not at eliminating poverty itself – too much aid money, we sense, actually goes to the rich in poor countries – but at stimulating development. We want a say in how foreign aid is used and we would prefer that it not be "tied aid," a policy that requires recipient countries to use the money to buy Canadian goods and services.

Looking back, it is clear that the 1980s marked the coming of age of Canada's global sensibilities. The decade taught us that we are part of an interdependent world, and that we can either attempt to play some larger role in shaping it – or have it shaped for us.

INTO THE NINETIES

Canada belongs to NATO, but Canadians know their country will never be a military superpower. Canada belongs to the Group of Seven, but Canadians know their country will always rank at or near the bottom of those seven major industrial nations. Our modest role on the global stage does not trouble us particularly. On the contrary, it helps define us: we are a middle power, occupying the middle ground between political or ideological extremes. In the 1990s, Ottawa may build on the international consciousness the nation developed in the 1980s, playing an expanded part in world affairs that Canadians would applaud: that of negotiators and arbitrators, peacekeepers and middle men in conflicts around the world. Such a role suits our sense of moral superiority – and indeed our identity. In fact, to be a true military power would only get in the way of that more honourable goal.

We are niche players, in both economic and military terms. We have to acknowledge that other nations make better shoes, textiles, and lawnmowers, and recognize that our real competitive advantage is our brain power. We can't outclass the Americans or the Japanese in manufacturing robotics, but we may be able to create computer software that makes them more efficient. In the 1990s, an increasing proportion of government and industrial policy will be directed at providing the training and education needed to exploit our native talents. The politician who can combine our economic and our moral ambitions will find a large measure of public favour.

Despite efforts to diversify, virtually every region of Canada is now economically dependent on a single sector: British Columbia on forestry, Alberta on oil and gas, Manitoba and Saskatchewan on agriculture, Ontario on automobiles, Quebec on hydro-electric power and the Maritimes on the fishery. But when Canadians are asked where the thrust of future policy initiatives should be directed, a stunning 55% say it should go in entirely new directions – that we should pursue an uncharted course. That statistic reflects an implicit recognition that to be hewers of wood and drawers of water won't work in the 1990s. Natural resources aren't enough. Sheer muscle isn't either. The answers – and the future – lie in new arenas: in aerospace, in computer programming, in biotechnology, in services. Again, the political leader who argues that Canada's best defence of its energy sector is not to hide oil and gas from foreign markets but to build the electric car will attract an impressive following.

Our global ambitions might also be satisfied in the decade ahead by the export of Canadian culture. In fact, contrary to the fears of anti-free-trade nationalists, it is the export of a nation's culture that best protects it. The Australians, consumed by their distance from the United States, understand this thesis – and it has made them aggressive sellers of their domestic cultural industries. Canadians, consumed by our proximity to the United States, have protected the arts. Australians conquer; we defend. And yet it often costs no more to make a film for foreign markets than it does for Canada alone. Free trade may foster a seminal change in Canadian attitudes, encouraging producers, filmmakers, and writers to display their talents around the world. We don't have to make films about Canadians; we have to make films with a Canadian perspective. It is that unique vision of the world that we must seek to export.

FACTS

Amount Canada gave in foreign aid to Africa in 1970: $37.4 million

Nation that received the most: Tunisia ($7.24 million)

Amount given to Africa in 1980: $285.7 million

Nation that received the most: Egypt ($27.8 million)

Amount given to Africa in 1988: $647.1 million

Nation that received the most: Egypt ($46.7 million)

"Will I have
a son? Will I
get married?
Will I be able
to emigrate
to Canada?"

QUESTIONS MOST FREQUENTLY ASKED
OF JOE YIP, A HONG KONG FORTUNE
TELLER, 1984

CIVIL WARS

ANGOLA: A Cuban-backed Marxist government versus the U.S.- and South-African-backed forces of UNITA. The war has been going on for 15 years. (See Namibia.)

COLOMBIA: The government of Virgilio Barco Vargas spent much of the decade fighting various left-wing guerrilla organizations as well as, in the late 1980s, the nation's powerful drug cartel.

ETHIOPIA: A Soviet-backed Marxist government versus regional liberation forces in Eritrea and Tigre. By the end of the decade, the government troops were reported to be near collapse.

EL SALVADOR: A 10-year conflict pitting left-wing guerrillas against a coalition government of Christian Democrats and right-wing political parties.

MOZAMBIQUE: The Marxist government against Renamo, a rebel force backed by South Africa. The war began in 1980 and continues.

NAMIBIA: The Marxist South West Africa People's Organization (SWAPO) against a South Africa-backed white minority government. A U.S.-brokered peace plan in 1988 promised to lead to black majority rule in Namibia in 1990, the withdrawal of South African troops and the withdrawal of Cuban troops from Angola in 1991.

NICARAGUA: The Marxist Sandinista government fought a 10-year war against U.S.-backed rebels, before ceding power in democratic elections in 1990.

SRI LANKA: The minority Tamils seek independence from the Sinhalese-dominated government.

THE SUDAN: After the fall of Nimeiry in 1985, the Muslim government in Khartoum engaged rebel forces in the south that were seeking independence. The conflict continues.

UGANDA: The National Resistance Army of Yoweri Musevni fought the military government of General Tito Okello and successfully seized power in Kampala in 1986.

COUPS OF THE EIGHTIES

Bangladesh, 1982

Bolivia, 1982

Burkina Fasso, 1980, 1982, 1983

Burundi, 1987

Paraguay, 1989

Central African Republic, 1981

Fiji, 1987

Ghana, 1981

Guatemala, 1982, 1983,
    1989 (attempt)

Guinea, 1984, 1985 (attempt)

Guinea-Bissau, 1980

Haiti, 1986, 1988 (twice)

Lesotho, 1986

Liberia, 1985 (attempt)

Nigeria, 1983, 1985

Philippines, 1986

Sudan, 1985, 1989

Surinam, 1982, 1981

South Yemen, 1986

Thailand, 1981 (attempt),
    1985 (attempt)

Uganda, 1985

COUNTRIES THAT CHANGED THEIR NAMES IN THE EIGHTIES

1982: Senegal and Gambia form a union for monetary and defence purposes known as Senegambia, but otherwise retain their independence

1984: Upper Volta becomes Burkino Fasso

1989: Burma becomes Myanmar, the name it had before British colonial rule

1988 OCT.

Canada wins a two-year term on the United Nations Security Council.

1989 APRIL

A contingent of 250 Canadian troops arrives in Namibia as part of a United Nations peacekeeping force, in advance of the country's independence.

1989 OCT.

Canada announces that it will join the 32-member Organization of American States, ending 17 years as a nation with observer status only.

FACTS

**Amount Canada gave to Central America and the Caribbean in 1980: $42.2 million
Nation that received the most: Jamaica ($7.8 million)
Amount Canada gave to Central America and the Caribbean in 1988: $158 million
Nation that received the most: Jamaica ($36 million)**

**Amount Canada gave to Asia in 1980: $234.6 million
Nation that received the most: Pakistan ($67.2 million)
Amount Canada gave to Asia in 1988: $506.2 million
Nation that received the most: Bangladesh ($133.5 million)**

"Canada is about the size of California and probably has a smaller gross national product. Perhaps Canada can be a prodder and a poker in trying to get Japan, West Germany and the United States to do a better job of managing the world economy. But clearly Canada is not going to dominate... Canada is a relatively small place by world standards."

LESTER THUROW, PROFESSOR OF ECONOMICS, MASSACHUSETTS INSTITUTE OF TECHNOLOGY, 1988

Ironically, the issue that helped concentrate our attention on international affairs is now in retreat. The collapse of the Communist order in Eastern Europe and the reunification of East and West Germany may yet bring crises or even civil wars, but the long shadow of nuclear Armageddon seems to have passed. As we enter the 1990s, two out of three Canadians believe that the demise of Communism, the end of the Cold War, and the subsequent nuclear and chemical arms-control agreements between the super-powers will yield a decade of peace. The dividend for Canada may be lower defence spending at home and abroad, although our NATO contribution is already so low that cutting it further might violate our formal commitments, to say nothing of our sense of moral obligation.

Militarily, our role in the 1990s will be as peacekeepers in the niche markets of Africa and the Middle East. Although Canadians would welcome an opportunity to play a greater role in solving international problems – apartheid in South Africa, the Arab-Israeli crisis, the lingering Protestant-Catholic wars in Northern Ireland – our presence at the bargaining table is not essential. And with the rapprochement of the Soviet Union and the United States, the need for third-party mediation is clearly diminishing.

Canada can exercise moral leadership more successfully in the quest to end poverty and famine in the Third World. Here, we might exploit our indigenous agricultural talents to develop new technologies that we can market internationally. Instead of merely selling wheat, we should export licences for new strains of drought-resistant grains. Instead of simply selling cattle, we should create immunization programs for cattle that would help feed the impoverished nations of the world. A national effort targeted in this direction would have widespread support. Canadians, it is worth remembering, were the largest per capita donors to the 1985 Live Aid concert.

But old habits die hard, and there is, simultaneously, a deep residual impulse in Canadians to seek protection from the economic threats posed by more powerful and more competitive nations. This sentiment was most evident during the free-trade debate of the 1980s. Before trade talks began, the public was overwhelmingly in favour of striking an agreement with the Americans. But by 1988, the percentage in favour of the deal had fallen from

94% to roughly 50% – evidence that Canadians feared they couldn't compete after all.

If advocates of a more outward-looking Canada fail to provide evidence in the 1990s that the rewards of dismantling the barriers to trade outweigh the risks, protectionist impulses may be resurrected. Many Canadians already regard the impact of the free-trade agreement on Canada as unfavourable. It is easy to be more pessimistic. Looking out at the powerful trading blocs now forming in Europe and Asia, some Canadians may conclude that competition, while desirable, is not possible – and that the answer is to protect what we already have. Even if the optimists win, and business, government, and public interests converge, the transition will be traumatic. A national collective effort will be required, affecting social policy on half a dozen fronts – from educational curricula to retraining the unemployed.

In the end, a reversion to insularity seems improbable. Not only are the opportunities almost without limit; most Canadians recognize intuitively that the old order, comfortable though it may have been, cannot be restored. Our choice in the 1990s is either to harness our talents and compete with the world, or to experience a steady decline in our standard of living and the world's esteem. And that is no choice at all.

FACTS

**Percentage of gross national product that Canada spent on foreign aid in 1980: .43
Percentage spent by the United States: .27
Percentage spent by France: .63
Percentage spent by Italy: .15**

**Percentage of gross national product Canada spent on foreign aid in 1987: .47
Percentage spent by the United States: .20
Percentage spent by France: .74
Percentage spent by Italy: .35**

**Estimated number of victims of terrorist incidents in the 1970s: 555
Estimated number in the 1980s: 1,000**

Fast Forward

CHAPTER 11

"If we don't solve our own problems, other people will. And the world of tomorrow belongs to the people who will solve them."

PIERRE ELLIOTT TRUDEAU, 1969

IN THE 1960S, THE FUTURIST HERMAN KAHN, ADDRESSING A conference in Toronto on the future of advertising, predicted the big issue in the years to come would be the population explosion. The marketing of birth-control devices, he concluded, would be a growth business. It is hard to imagine, twenty-five years later, how anyone could be both so wrong and so right. Kahn's forecasts were made in the midst of the baby boom. He didn't foresee the change in values that would cause the birth rate to plummet in the 1970s. Nor could he have foreseen the impact that the fear of AIDS would have on sexual behaviour in the 1980s. Still, if he were alive today he would appreciate the irony: increasingly monogamous, increasingly celibate, we sit in front of our television sets watching advertisements promoting the use of condoms.

Predicting the future is a risky business at best. In the profession of survey research it is conventional wisdom that polling cannot be used to predict behaviour in the absence of knowledge of events that might cause it to change. But you don't have to be a pollster to understand that unexpected events can influence behaviour in ways that defy prediction; it's just common sense. Alvin Toffler uses waves as an analogy to explain the tenuous relationship between the present and the future. Current trends have a force of their own, he says, which carries them, like waves, toward the beach. When the force dissipates new trends surface, but like new waves they take shape in the wash of old ones. The limitations of forecasting are all too often forgotten. In the interests of provocation, current trends are drawn like straight lines into the future as if they could reveal its shape, whereas in fact they can only hint at it.

Still, there are forces at work in Canada today which properly understood offer us clues about the decade ahead. The most obvious are demographic, and the most significant of these is the Big Generation. The progeny of the post-war baby boom between 1946 and 1964 will continue to dramatically reshape Canadian society throughout the 1990s. Much has been said about the aging of the baby boomers: their sheer numbers will undermine the actuarial foundations of the Canada Pension Plan and overwhelm the health-care system; as the last of them enter their early middle years in the mid-1990s, the bottom will fall out of the new housing market. But this is straight-line extrapolation. What is more certain is that in the decade ahead we will see not only more older people, but also a new type of older person.

Twenty years ago, Mick Jagger scoffed at the suggestion that he might still be singing "Satisfaction" when he was 40; but that is precisely what he was doing in the summer of 1990 at the stately age of 46. In the 1960s, Jean Shrimpton was told that at the tender age of 21 she was too old to continue modelling; twenty-five years later, the glamour girls on the covers of the supermarket tabloids include such spring chickens as Cheryl Tiegs, Linda Evans, and Joan Collins. As the Big Generation has grown older, it has redefined the concepts of youth, beauty, and acceptable social behaviour in its own image. It has transformed society's role models from spry 20-year-olds to seemingly ageless 40-year-olds. "Fat and happy," a euphemism for growing old in the 1960s, is now an oxymoron.

The Big Generation was brought up to believe that progress was normal. It was taught that if you worked hard you could be anything you wanted to be and that education was the key to success. As a consequence, it is the best-educated generation in history, and many of its constituents would describe themselves as "workaholics." Yet many would also admit that they are not what they want to be. Their experience contradicts the values on which they were raised, and this conflict has produced a pattern of inherent disloyalty and constant experimentation. The phenomenon John Naisbitt calls "the Baskin and Robbinization" of North America – where the norm was once three flavours it is now thirty-one – is the result of the baby boomers' insistence on choice. They don't believe in the old ways because the old ways have often failed them. They believe in their ability to choose new ways, and if their choices prove wrong they simply move on to the next one.

The 1960s celebrated youth, the 1980s middle age. In the 1990s, as they achieve numerical superiority, it is the elderly who will enjoy special status. Society will treat them differently, and they will behave differently. The process has already begun. Twenty years ago, half the people living in poverty were over 65 years of age; in 1990 the proportion is less than 15 percent. To the aging baby boomers the problems of the Canada Pension Plan will seem less catastrophic, as financial institutions introduce more new retirement-savings products and employers use private pension coverage as an inducement to maintain a dwindling and aging employment base. In response to the demands of a more affluent elderly population, the health-care system will shift its focus from sickness to wellness, making the practice of medicine more preventive and less curative. Housing starts may decline, but the senior citizens of the Big Generation will have accumulated three trillion dollars in residential real estate which will eventually find its way back into the economy.

Another demographic phenomenon of the past twenty-five years, the acceleration of female participation in the workplace, is generally associated with macroeconomic conditions: as inflation eroded income, the family required two incomes. But in fact female participation rates are a reflection less of economic variables than of educational attainment. The Big Generation is the only generation that has ever experienced something close to an egalitarian education system. Women now represent more than two-thirds of all post-secondary enrolment in the humanities, education, and the arts. By the end of the decade they will probably dominate the faculties of law, medicine, and business. An educational revolution has made the working woman, not an economic aberration, but a fact of life. Indeed, it is not far-fetched to suggest that within the next twenty years women will achieve parity in the labour force. Women's issues, often treated as lesbian-inspired irritants by politicians and employers, are merely the tip of a very large iceberg. Looking ahead, universal child care, flex-time and spousal employment (where a man and woman are hired as a package) seem inevitable. On the other hand, sexual stereotyping and sexual harassment will soon vanish as serious issues, having become as socially acceptable as chewing tobacco.

The prospect of greater female participation in the work-place makes unlikely any upturn in the birth rate. In fact, it is pos-sible that within the next ten years the country's population will decline. The conclusion is obvious: to sustain economic growth in the 1990s Canada will need more immigration. In the mid-1980s, we accepted 75,000 immigrants a year; by the end of the decade the number had risen to approximately 175,000. Simply to maintain our current population we will soon require an annual net immigration of 200,000. Where will these new Canadians come from? The nature of Canadian immigration has changed remarkably in twenty-five years. The United States and Europe once accounted for 85 percent of immigrants to Canada, but the proportion has declined to less than 25 percent. The majority now come from Third World and developing countries. This, too, is a fact of life, and it means that visible minorities will play a more prominent role in shaping the Canadian mosaic in the 1990s. Their impact is already apparent in the larger urban centres, where there is growing racial unrest.

Looking at these demographic transformations, breathtaking in their magnitude and force, it is easy to envisage the 1990s as being very different from the decade from which we have recently emerged. The fact that they are accompanied by equally profound shifts in public opinion makes the prospect of dramatic change in the decade ahead a certainty.

In terms of our state of mind, we appear to be entering a new epoch. In the years of peace and prosperity since the Second World War, Canadians were preoccupied with the pursuit of mate-rial possessions. This began to change in the late 1980s, as people began to attach more importance to the quality of their lives. And the evidence suggests that this attitudinal shift – from wanting "more" to wanting "better" – is here to stay. The popularization of the environment as a public issue is perhaps the best indication, but there are others. Indeed, a whole array of social concerns will dominate political discourse in the 1990s. Health, nutrition, illicit drugs, urban violence, the antisocial behaviour of young people: any or all of these issues could rise to the top of the public agenda in the 1990s.

As with all emerging trends, there is no simple explanation for this new commitment to quality of life. In part it's a response to involuntary risk. People sense that, despite their new-found affluence, they now confront perils beyond their control. Cholesterol, chlorofluorocarbons, meltdown, swarming, crack – these are just a few of the words that make up a vocabulary of fear that didn't exist in the 1960s. Portable telephones, VCRs, luxury cars, and designer jeans are to some extent insulation against such threats. But it is apparent that many Canadians have begun to ask themselves whether we have not paid too high a price for progress – and, indeed, if it was the pursuit of material possessions that led us to this accumulation of risk. People now yearn for a "kinder and gentler" life in which quality is valued over quantity and morality is a more important consideration in decision-making. In the 1990s they will oppose anyone who strives for progress at all cost. Even today, anyone who wants to divert a river or erect an office tower must overcome the public sentiment that "enough is enough."

This pro-quality, anti-development point of view will lead us in the 1990s into a prolonged period of introspection. On the one hand, we continue to see ourselves as more tolerant, charitable, and peaceable than, if not the rest of the world, then certainly the United States. On the other hand, our growing concern about the quality of our lives suggests to us that we may be less tolerant, charitable, and peaceable than we thought. In short, our image of ourselves is increasingly in conflict with our day-to-day experience. Something will have to give, because in this post-free-trade period our desire to maintain our uniqueness vis-à-vis the United States has grown even stronger. Clearly, we will have to alter either the way we see ourselves or the way we live. The focus of this introspection will be urban. How do we make our cities more livable? Many Canadians will conclude that urban life styles must undergo significant modification in the 1990s. But they will do so with great reluctance, because the prospect of change, exciting in the 1980s, is now frightening.

Move ahead into uncharted waters or turn back in search of a more familiar course – this will be the central philosophical debate in Canadian politics in the next decade. Assuming, of course, that anyone is listening. Canadians now harbour serious doubts about the political process as a mechanism for the resolution of social conflict. It began in the 1980s as opposition to government intervention in the economy; people came to the conclusion that government intrusion in the private sector had had negative consequences for the economy. Even in circumstances in which government intervention was desirable, it often seemed ineffective; why are there no fewer single mothers on welfare today than there were thirty years ago? Skepticism about the efficacy of government led eventually to an unprecedented loss of confidence in the people in charge, the politicians, which is certain to have a lasting effect in the 1990s.

But how does a society come to grips with problems such as ozone depletion, crime in the streets, and affordable housing when it has lost faith in its problem-solvers? A promising option is the concept of "partnerships" between the public, private, and volunteer sectors. Government still sets the priorities, but business provides the expertise and technical assistance, and volunteer and community groups provide the execution. While examples of such partnerships are still few and far between, they have been remarkably successful. There could be many more of them in the decade ahead if the public renews its commitment to voluntarism and business comes to the realization that it has an economic stake in the welfare of the community.

And how will we resolve the greatest of our problems: the future of the Canadian federation? Was the failure of the Meech Lake Accord evidence that Canadians have also lost faith in the country? In the end, the issue that determined the outcome of the Meech Lake debate was Quebec. English Canada saw the Accord as yet another concession to Quebec's demands for special treatment. Quebec saw the Accord as little more than acknowledgement of the fact of its cultural distinctiveness. English Canadians saw unanimous, federal government support for the Accord as a signal that fair play was a thing of the past. Quebec saw public opposition to the Accord as a signal that English Canada was unprepared to accommodate its cultural aspirations. Neither side felt any sense of risk. English Canadians refused to accept that the failure of the accord would have any lasting consequences for the country; they didn't believe Quebec would separate, or that it could survive if it did. Quebeckers entertained no such doubts; with new-found faith in their entrepreneurial skills, they felt confident that if pushed they could make it on their own.

Emotionally, Quebec has now made its exit. With the demise of the Meech Lake Accord, Quebeckers closed one chapter and began a new one in which they will play a more autonomous, if still undefined, role. Quebec knows what it wants; now it's English Canada that's confused. But change will come slowly. It serves the short-term interests of both Brian Mulroney and Robert Bourassa to prolong the metamorphosis from which a more independent Quebec will emerge. In the case of the prime minister of Canada, because as the nation's leader he must make every effort to hold it together. In the case of the premier of Quebec, because he must eventually differentiate himself from his separatist opposition. He can't support federalism; but when Quebeckers come to the realization that a premature separation would have negative consequences for the province, he can fight an election on his record as an economic leader. In the meantime, Quebec will negotiate with Ottawa. And with every new bilateral agreement, English Canadians will be less inclined to accommodate Quebec's interests. Instead, the other nine provinces are likely to take a "what about us?" position and press their own agendas more vigorously.

Where will this take us? We can rule out at least two eventualities. The first is a return to federalism as we have known it; Quebec is now too committed to change. The second is any arrangement in which sovereignty-association is granted only to Quebec; no federal government could survive the political backlash in English Canada. Perhaps the most likely scenario is the evolution of a structure similar to Switzerland's: five strong cantons representing separate cultures, governing in the interests of those cultures, with a federal government that is little more than the instrument of their collective commercial interests. Canada as Switzerland? It is only speculation, of course. And given the state of public opinion as we begin the 1990s, it may even be optimistic.